Treatment of Special Populations with Ericksonian Approaches

Ericksonian Monographs

Treatment of Special Populations with Ericksonian Approaches

Edited by Stephen R. Lankton
and Jeffrey K. Zeig

Brunner/Mazel Publishers   •   New York

LIBRARY OF CONGRESS

Library of Congress Cataloging-in-Publication Data

Treatment of special populations with Ericksonian approaches / edited
   by Stephen R. Lankton and Jeffrey K. Zeig.
         p.   cm. — (Ericksonian monographs : no. 3)
   Includes bibliographies.
   ISBN 0-87630-494-3
   1. Hypnotism—Therapeutic use.   2. Psychotherapy.   3. Erickson,
Milton H.   I. Lankton, Stephen R.   II. Zeig, Jeffrey K., 1947–
III. Series.
   [DNLM: 1. Erickson, Milton H.   2. Hypnosis.   3. Psychotherapy.
W1 ER44 no. 3 / WM 415 T784]
RC495.T74 1988
616.89'06512 — dc 19
DNLM/DLC
for Library of Congress

                                                                                          87-35514
                                                                                          CIP

Copyright © 1988 by The Milton H. Erickson Foundation

Published by
BRUNNER/MAZEL, INC.
19 Union Square
New York, NY 10003

MANUFACTURED IN THE UNITED STATES OF AMERICA

10   9   8   7   6   5   4   3   2   1

Ericksonian Monographs

Ericksonian Monographs publishes only original manuscripts dealing with Ericksonian approaches to hypnosis, family therapy, and psychotherapy, including techniques, case studies, research and theory.

The *Monographs* will publish only those articles of highest quality that foster the growth and development of the Ericksonian approach and exemplify an original contribution to the fields of physical and mental health. In keeping with the purpose of the *Monographs*, articles should be prepared so that they are readable to a heterogeneous audience of professionals in psychology, medicine, social work, dentistry and related clinical fields.

Abstracts of each article are on file at the Milton H. Erickson Foundation, Inc., in the following languages: French, German, Italian, and Spanish.

Publication of the *Ericksonian Monographs* shall be on an irregular basis; no more than three times per year. The Monographs are a numbered, periodical publication. Dates of publication are determined by the quantity of high quality articles accepted by the Editorial Board and the Board of Directors of the Milton H. Erickson Foundation, Inc., rather than calendar dates.

Manuscripts should be *submitted in quintuplicate* (5 copies) with a 100–150-word abstract to Stephen R. Lankton, M.S.W., P.O. Box 958, Gulf Breeze, Florida 32561-0958. Manuscripts of length ranging from 15 to 100 typed double-spaced pages will be considered for publication. Submitted manuscripts cannot be returned to authors. Authors with telecommunication capability may presubmit one copy electronically in either 1200 or 300 baud rate and the following communication parameters: 8 bit word size, No parity, 1 stop bit, x-on/x-off enabled, ASCII and xmodem transfer protocols are acceptable. Call (904) 932-6819 to arrange transmission and security passwords.

Style and format of submitted manuscripts must adhere to instructions described in the *Publication Manual of the American Psychological Association*

(3rd edition, 1983). The manuscripts will be returned for revision if reference citations, preparation of tables and figures, manuscript format, avoidance of sexist language, copyright permission for cited material, title page style, etc. do not conform to the *Manual*.

Copyright ownership must be transferred to the Milton H. Erickson Foundation, Inc., if your manuscript is accepted for publication. The Editor's acceptance letter will include a form explaining copyright release, ownership and privileges.

Reference citations should be scrutinized with special care to credit originality and avoid plagiarism. Referenced material should be carefully checked by the author prior to first submission of the manuscript.

Charts and photographs accompanying the manuscripts must be presented in camera-ready form.

Copy editing and galley proofs will be sent to the authors for revisions. Manuscripts must be submitted in clearly written, acceptable, scholarly English. Neither the Editor nor the Publisher is responsible for correcting errors of spelling and grammar: the manuscript, after acceptance, should be immediately ready for publication. Authors should understand there will be a charge passed on to them by the Publisher for revision of galleys.

Prescreening and review procedures for articles is outlined below. Priority is given to those articles which conform to the designated theme for the upcoming *Monographs*. All manuscripts will be prescreened, absented of the author's name, by the Editor or one member of the Editorial Board and one member of either the Continuing Medical Education Committee or the Board of Directors of the Milton H. Erickson Foundation, Inc.

Final acceptance of all articles is done at the discretion of the Board of Directors of the Milton H. Erickson Foundation, Inc. Their decisions will be made after acceptable prescreened articles have been reviewed and edited by a minimum of four persons: two Editorial Board members, one member of the CME Committee or the Board of Directors, and the Editor. Occasionally, reviewers selected by the Editor will assist in compiling feedback to authors.

Feedback for authors and manuscript revision will be handled by the Editor usually between one and two months after submission of the prepared manuscript. Additional inquiries are welcomed if addressed to the Editor.

Contents

Articles

Contributors

Gordon Dean Bathel, A.C.S.W.
Clinical Supervisor, O'Rielly Care Center, and in private practice in Tucson, Arizona

Carlos Ronaldo Carreon, A.C.S.W.
Regional Clinical Supervisor, Human Affairs International, and in private practice in Tucson, Arizona

John H. Edgette, Psy.D.
Director, The Milton H. Erickson Institute of Philadelphia, and in private practice

Claude Millette, M.S.W.
Social Worker in Toronto, Ontario, Canada

Keiichi Miyata, M.A.
Associate Professor, Department of Education, Niigata University, Japan

John A. Moran, Ph.D.
Independent practice in Scottsdale, Arizona

Susan Mullarky, M.A.
Private practice in Bothell, Washington

Noelle M. Poncelet, Ph.D.
On the clinical faculty at the University of California at San Francisco, Department of Community Medicine, and at Stanford University, Department of Psychiatry and Behavioral Sciences, and in private practice in San Francisco and Menlo Park

Madeleine M. Richeport, Ph.D.
Affiliated with the Office of Transcultural Education and Research, Department of Psychiatry, University of Miami School of Medicine, and the Mental Health Secretariat, Commonwealth of Puerto Rico

Thomas L. South, Ph.D.
Clinical counselor, The Counseling Center, University of Dayton, Ohio

Bernhard Trenkle, Dipl. Psych.
Director of Milton Erickson Institute of Heidelberg, Rottweil, and editor of the newsletter of the Milton Erickson Society of Germany

Mark Franchot Weiss, Ph.D.
Director, The Milton H. Erickson Institute of Northern Illinois and in private practice in Chicago

Introduction

This special volume of the Ericksonian Monographs contains unpublished "accepted papers" from the Third International Congress on Ericksonian Approaches to Hypnosis and Psychotherapy held in Phoenix, Arizona, December 3–7, 1986. The papers contained here are a part of this special volume only and will not be found in the *Proceedings of the Third International Congress*. Jeffrey K. Zeig organized the Congress, and, he and I share the editorship of this special volume. We are excited about accumulating in one easily acquired volume the following eleven chapters which depict the use of Ericksonian methods for various special treatment populations. A creative application of Erickson's ideas, as is here exemplified by the treatment of various difficult cases, is of utmost importance to clinicians. This set of presentations for the International Congress is certain to stimulate creative sparks among readers.

The chapters illustrate cases and techniques dealing with clients who come with phobias, pain, stuttering, autism, psychosis, and multiple personality. They include some timely and far reaching concerns such as those brought by homosexual clients and Mexican American populations and other cross-cultural groups.

Marc F. Weiss' chapter, "Ericksonian Hypnotherapy as Surgical Analgesia in an Exploratory and Operative Cancer Procedure: The Patient's Experiences and Reflections," describes the treatment and presents a follow-up interview. It is an unusual and educational account because the personal reflections of the client have been recorded. Thomas South presents his account of pain control, healing, and resulting amnesias in "Hypnosis in Childbirth: A Case Study in Anesthesia." Although a cesarean birth unexpectedly interrupted the planned delivery, the results are remarkable. Noelle Poncelet, in "Pain and Pleasure: Awareness and Trust," provides techniques that help people focus on the pleasures of living rather than the agony of pain. Her approach is drawn from a study of individuals who were successfully dealing with pain and, as such, it is distinguished from the perhaps all too common studies drawn from malachievement and partial failure.

"Presenting Ideas to Phobics" by John A. Moran provides a fresh look at a very large population which can profit from application of fundamental principles such as using social systems, confusion, and activity in the therapy. He gives basic and systematic guidelines for beginning therapy and proceeding successfully with most phobic clients. Similarly, "Charles Van Riper Meets Milton H. Erickson: Approaches in the Treatment of the Adult Stutterer" by Bernhard Trenkle brings creative ideas for working with the often unspoken therapy of stuttering. But more, Mr. Trenkle reveals the man behind the work who bore uncanny similarity to Dr. Erickson in his own area of specialization. The comparison between Van Riper and Erickson helps to broaden our understanding of the realistic application of Erickson's principles of treatment.

Susan Mullarky writes "A 'Lavender Duster' Considers the 'Purple Sage': Ericksonian Approaches with Homosexuals and Lesbians" to show special concerns in the treatment of life issues as they effect homosexuals and lesbians. Her account is built from both personal and professional insights, and its strength lies in how her model of honesty and sincerity invites us each to do the same. "The Application of Ericksonian Approaches to Autistic Children" by Keiichi Miyata traces the successful treatment of an autistic child by the use of paradoxical symptom prescription and symptom substitution. Remarkably, the persistent use of these Ericksonian interventions alone alleviated the distressing childhood symptomatology.

"Dangerous to Self and Others: The Management of Acute Psychosis Using Ericksonian Techniques of Hypnosis and Hypnotherapy" by John H. Edgette reveals one doctor's use of hypnotic techniques with a hospitalized population displaying active psychotic behavior. With creativity and confidence Dr. Edgette has repeatedly managed potentially dangerous episodes and turned them into therapeutic situations. Claude Millette treated a self-mutilating client diagnosed as multiple personality using an approach which combined hypnosis, visual hallucination and dialogue. His case report is entitled "Using Subparts in a Case of Multiple Personality." Excerpts from the client's journal were used to demonstrate progress in the therapy.

G. Dean Bathel and Carlos R. Carreon, in "Cross-Cultural Ericksonian Techniques with Mexican-American Clients," examine historical and cultural aspects of work with this client population. They trace some of the roots of multigenerational non-blood kinship ties and the importance of being sensitive to and employing these ties in therapy. Madeleine M. Richeport provides the expertise of an anthropologist in "Transcultural Issues in Ericksonian Hypnotherapy." She calls for a shift from a unicultural to a transcultural posture and outlines other guidelines to help develop culturally sensitive therapy.

Case reports of work with specialized populations excites me and brings home the awareness that Ericksonian approaches to therapy have reached a very wide professional venue. I expect that, like the Third International Congress on Ericksonian Approaches to Psychotherapy, this special volume of the Ericksonian Monographs will be a resource of great value and practical inspiration.

Stephen R. Lankton
Gulf Breeze, FL
May 21, 1987

Ericksonian Hypnotherapy as Surgical Analgesia in an Exploratory and Operative Cancer Procedure: The Patient's Experiences and Reflections

Marc Franchot Weiss, Ph.D.

Marc Franchot Weiss, Ph.D. (Illinois Institute of Technology) is Director of The Milton H. Erickson Institute of Northern Illinois and is in private practice in Chicago. Previous publications include research studies on the treatment of insomnia and the development of children's attitudes toward mental illness.

Weiss shares a case of surgical analgesia in cancer surgery. In a most unusual and captivating interview, he discusses the client's reaction to a range of questions from the experience of the hypnotic sessions to the ethics of treatment and the conduct of the medical staff.

While research has supported claims for the effectiveness of hypnosis as an analgesic, anesthetic and pain control in obstetrics, dentistry, oncology and surgery, there continues to be a reluctance in the medical community to employ nonpharmaceutical agents for pain amelioration and control. Perhaps, this reluctance is attributable to malpractice and litigation concerns or to the continued and increasing emphasis on "biological" rather than "holistic" medicine. Dr. Erickson's (1966a) observation still seems to be true: "Today only a sporadic application of hypnosis for surgical anesthesia is reported. It is also unfortunate that the advent of chloroform, ether, and nitrous oxide during the middle of the last century relegated hypnosis to undeserved obscurity and prevented it from being used as an anesthetic agent."

Address reprint requests to Marc F. Weiss, Ph.D., 6640 N. Maplewood Ave., Chicago, IL 60645.

The following case presentation offers the experiences, successful hypnotherapeutic treatment, anecdotes and reflections of a 40-year-old female, type two diabetic, who sought hypnosis for the purpose of surgical analgesia used during a coninization (cone biopsy) for carcinoma in situ (cancer in the cervical epiphelia cells). Detailed are the patient's experiences during the hypnotic sessions, reflections on differences between Ericksonian and traditional/directive approaches, and experiences prior to, during and following surgery. Much of this information is based upon interview data 6 and 12 months following the successful surgery.

Coninization has become a more common and less radical procedure than a hysterectomy. Lois had been to four practitioners who, as she stated, "failed" to hypnotize her with traditional techniques. A freelance writer and avid psychology and medical researcher, she stumbled upon the Ericksonian approach. Finding it more acceptable than traditional directive approaches, Lois specifically sought out an Ericksonian hypnotist. Initially, she would not elaborate on her need for hypnosis rather than the preferred and standard use of anesthesia. Lois indicated that she was worried about transfusions and other medical problems; the interview was at the beginning of the AIDS (Acquired Immune Deficiency Syndrome) scare. She had been engaged with another therapist in traditional analytic psychotherapy for approximately one year with three sessions a week. Surgery had already been scheduled for two weeks after the initial hypnotherapy appointment.

Diagnostic Parameters

Based upon her interaction style, information provided and concealed, ongoing responsiveness and resistance, and Leary's (1957) interpersonal checklist, it was hypothesized that Lois was quite independent, uncooperative, somewhat distrustful, somewhat resistant, and self-effacing or self-deprecating. She did not want to be dependent on others and avoided any show of weaknesses. Control was seen as a major issue. Only if confidence was gained would she follow someone else's lead and/or direction. She wanted the hypnotic procedure to work but only in a manner and at a time that was acceptable to her. Her meaning seemed to be "I dare you to accomplish what I want you to accomplish." She had become a pseudo-expert on hypnosis and Milton Erickson and mustered all her strength to have control over the therapist.

Lois was intelligent and, to some extent, an intellectualizer. She was internally focused and primarily visual in her mode of processing sensory information. She wanted to be "one up" and continually strived for that position. She communicated in thoughts and feelings. She preferred symbolic and metaphorical communication. Insight and knowledge were sought after and valued. She presented herself in a somewhat seductive manner and frequently made sexual references and innuendos. Given her need to control situations and maintain a "one up" position, traditional, directive, authoritarian approaches failed. The key elements in the successful treatment was the use of indirection, multiple meanings, and metaphorical communication that allowed her to be in control and to use what she wanted. She was able to pick and choose and use what was relevant to her own needs, goals and understandings.

Treatment

Since I would be absent when the surgical procedure was conducted, it was reasoned that Lois needed a series of resources so that she could induce or control the trance herself. She should be able to be aware of any pain or discomfort during the surgical procedure as she needed or wanted. It was reasoned that a situation could arise where her physical and/or emotional safety and well-being could be jeopardized and that she might, at some point, need to be aware of pain in order to properly respond. Resources were elicited over the first four sessions through the use of trance phenomena and a series of metaphors which are outlined below. The resources included the ability to move the pain or sensation location, and/or to have it in one or many spots; the ability to split the pain into components; full or selective amnesia; dissociation; pseudo-orientation in time; time distortion; and positive and negative hallucinations. The remaining sessions served as reinforcers of her ability to utilize those resources.

Treatment consisted of a series of nine hypnotherapeutic sessions. The total time spent was 12 hours. At the patient's request, one of the sessions was held approximately one hour before surgery. The therapy was Ericksonian with emphasis on the multiple embedded metaphor structure (Lankton & Lankton, 1983). This form was modified by the circular metaphor model delivery pattern (Weiss, 1986). This metaphorical therapy included indirect suggestions and binds to achieve hypnotic analgesia through time distortion, amnesia, dissociation, attitude change, and pain reinterpretation (i.e., the notion of the tickling feather rather than the cutting knife). Initially, Lois was quite reluctant to enter into trance; therefore, paradoxical techniques, a refusal on my part to initiate the trance process, and a series of stories (e.g., how Dr. Erickson would put himself into trance to treat his own pain, what Dr. Erickson would do to induce trance in resistant subjects) were used.

At one point during the second session Lois became so impatient with "waiting to go into trance" that she initiated trance herself. During the third session, she became so frustrated with my level of indirection that she asked me to be more directive and take more control. She stated that she was coming to me for help and it was time for me to become more active.

While in trance during the fourth session, she asked for "the test." Initially, I would softly rub her arms, fingers, and palms with various objects from neuropsychological testing materials such as a sharp tooth comb or pins. In subsequent sessions, she was allowed to do her own testing with her eyes open. Other materials carefully employed were nails, screws and razor blades. During these sessions, there was constant and simultaneous mention of feathers and tickling. She was asked if she could feel the tickling feathers while the sharp objects were pushed into or scraped along her skin. Many times during these sessions she would laugh and mutter about the feathers and how she was ticklish. On one occasion, she literally pushed a long pin through her hand and was able to control bleeding. Lois wanted it to be perfect and would only accept in-office experimentation as proof. At the fifth session, it was obvious to me that her dream would be fulfilled; however, the patient insisted on further reinforcement and experimentation/practice with needles, etc.

A series of metaphors using various themes were employed. While some were intentionally affect, behavior, or attitude metaphors (Lankton & Lankton, 1983, 1986), there were many cases in which there was great overlap. Language and terminology had multiple levels of meaning. Examples included:

1. A metaphor using a play on words about a coninization. Making ice cream cones and sometimes to make it better they would have to cut out certain parts so that people would not get cancer. Making the ice cream cone safe was called a cone-ice-ation.
2. Her name which also is a homonym for an occupation was used: the Smith who felt no pain when he accidentally cut his finger while shoeing a horse.
3. A metaphor describing the development of self-confidence in an individual.
4. A metaphor describing the development of confidence and trust in others.
5. A metaphor about relief following the ending of a dreaded life experience.
6. Dr. Erickson's boiler story (Erickson & Rossi, 1979).
7. Erickson's story about the lady with the tiger under the bed (Lustig, 1975).

8. Erickson's good-bye story (Lankton & Lankton, 1986).
9. A metaphor about how people protect their own interests.
10. A story about how Jesus Christ felt no pain and was able to control bleeding at the crucifixion.
11. A story about soldiers winning a battle that no one thought they could win, especially since they did it in an unusual way without the standard weapons. Instead of knives, they used their mental powers and concentration.
12. A metaphor about two football teams. One team had many injuries and the other had no injuries. The injured team did not notice the pain and finished the game with a successful victory.
13. A multipurpose metaphor about how a young man who was studying to be a bullfighter learned confidence fighting the feared bull. He also feared being in crowds but he did not even notice the crowds and noise when he was concentrating on the bull.
14. A story about the watchmaker who had to do perfect repairs, but with deteriorating eyesight, relinquished his job and skill to a younger, less perfect apprentice.
15. Erickson's story about Joe and the tomato plant (Erickson, 1966b).
16. A modification of the Lanktons' story of the healer within (Lankton & Lankton, 1983).
17. A story about how sometimes things turn out contrary to others' expectations, but consistent with one's own hopes.
18. A story about my own oral surgery and how the staff had to stop the administration of sodium pentothal during the procedure. I responded by imaging that the drilling crew was drilling in the street outside.

While many concepts and suggestions were embedded during the delivery of metaphors, the intent was to emphasize five areas: 1) how people can alter their own experience to protect their own interests; 2) how people can have minimal bleeding and heal rapidly; 3) how unpleasant sensations can be handled with comfort; 4) how people can alter concentration and attention and focus on some things and not on others; 5) how one can see the smile on the faces of people who said, "It cannot be done."

An ambiguous function assignment (Lankton, 1984; Lankton & Lankton, 1986) was utilized. The assignment was to walk her dog and put the leash tightly around her arm. Lois was asked to think about why I would ask her to do such a crazy thing. Onto this situation she projected that she could feel no sensation and still control and protect a valuable life and/or possession. She also indicated that she could still feel pressure, the pull on her arm, and so, if need be, she could be aware of potential harm.

A kinesthetic-based reinduction signal (or anchor) was created so that she could control and induce trance. During the surgical procedure she, of her own accord, asked the anesthesiologist to push, in a pulsating manner, a specific spot (the anchor) on her right wrist.

Pre- and postoperative suggestions relative to how to handle the postoperative aspects of the surgery and any anticipatory anxiety prior to surgery were used. Potential phobic or anxiety responses related aspects to the operating and preoperative waiting rooms were included with these suggestions. Finally, it was implied that "pain control" would essentially be a one-time occurrence, but that, if need be, it could be re-created in other situations only through conscious control and awareness, and only after consideration was given to personal safety. That is, if pain was life-threatening, she would "know" that medical assistance was needed.

Case Incidents

On the day of the surgery, Lois looked and acted almost as if she were intoxicated or on amphetamines. She was so high with excitement that I decided to act in a distracting manner so the surgical staff would not notice her behavior had changed after a few short moments with me. I hypothesized that if they questioned her behavior and affect that they would suspect something was wrong and perhaps postpone the surgery.

As indicated above, the key element in her treatment was the amount of indirection, multiple meanings and metaphorical communication. To this date, when we speak, she assumes that everything I say is metaphorical and has multiple meanings. For example, when talking with Lois on the phone approximately four months later and talking about when we would get together to do the interview for this chapter, I stated, "Right now it would be hard to pin me down on a date." She reported looking to see if the pin which we had used during the presurgical trials was still in her hand. She seemed to believe that she or I might have left the pin in her hand and that she had gained such control over pain that it might still be there for all those months and that she would not have known about it. Soon after she inquired if I would hypnotize her to "free herself up" for her other therapy. I questioned simply, "Why don't you let me cure you?" Shortly thereafter she terminated that therapy and had done well without continued therapy or further "official" hypnotherapy. I have maintained contact and at times during a phone chat, with or without my own awareness, I may have mentioned something which could be construed as hypnotherapeutic.

The Patient's Experiences and Reflections

Following the exploratory and operative cancer procedure, Lois was quite willing to discuss everything and anything in detail. The information provided was based on a series of interviews approximately one week after surgery and six and twelve months after surgery. Some information was given prior to and during the treatment, but was reiterated for the purposes of this paper. The complete interview lasted several hours and has been edited and organized for clarity. Unless otherwise noted (e.g., parenthetical statements), it is to be assumed that all statements are direct quotes. Lois's own words perhaps best exemplify and describe the differences, philosophy, goals, and nature of Ericksonian hypnotherapy.

Weiss: Why was hypnosis rather than general anesthesia chosen?

Lois: I was to have a coninization, a cone biopsy for carcinoma in situ, cancer of the epiphelial cells, here in the cervix. It is an investigative, possibly curative procedure, a surgical procedure to remove any existing cancer cells.

Weiss: Was it cancer?

Lois: It was cancer. [It] was carcinoma and four months later [I had] no cancer. I did not want to go under general anesthesia, not only because of acknowledged risks of general anesthesia to the population at large but, because I have some minor medical problems without [the side effects of] general anesthesia.

Weiss: What problems were those?

Lois: The medical problems…I had high ANA associated with, this was atypically high, with Lupus and some inflammatory arthritic disease, rheumatoid arthritis. I prefer natural or holistic approaches. I'm a type two diabetic. Had this for eight years. It's controlled and I was in good health.

Weiss: Given the legal, malpractice, surgical and medical implications, what did the doctors say?

Lois: When I asked [about alternative analgesic methods, I] approached them about the various options. They did a coposcopy [outpatient procedure]. They would look into [the] vaginal area, etc. They could not see the full extent [of the cancer]. They had to look further. I wanted one procedure. They said they always do [this procedure] by general anesthesia. The option was with a spinal. I asked was there any way with [a] local? [They said it is a] rare occurrence this way. I [said I] really would like to try that way, but I would [only want to] have a general there if needed. I did not want [a general] unless it was life threatening. They agreed to that, [but they indicated that the] local was not recommended because of pain during procedure. I was [anticipating] anxiety and phobic reactions relative to the general and [its] trappings. I wanted to be [at my] emotionally strongest, five days after [the surgical] period. I wanted a separate appointment with the anesthesiology consultant. Someone who could explain [the] entire procedure. I found the anesthesiologist reluctant [to consider alternate methods]. I'm a person who needs to KNOW [everything that could or would happen as well as all the negative things]. I did *not* want a general, I wanted it more natural.

Weiss: How did you get referred to me?

Lois: I contacted [a well respected national organization for professional and clinical hypnosis] and explained [what I wanted] and they gave a list of members. I went to two [hypnotherapists] recommended by [mental health professionals] I respected. They were ineffective because I was put through passive relaxation exercises, such as in yoga classes, and then could do my own and achieved deep relaxation and did not find what I wanted for me, what I perceived to be hypnosis. I was not in a suggestible stage. I did imagine pretty scenes. I investigated it...it was standard textbook procedure, technique type stuff. Even though I was cooperating, I did not feel it was effective. I had a fear of hypnosis. I was afraid because, I had this unrealistic picture. I did not know what was going on. The fear diminished with time. Hypnosis was an element in some of them. I was afraid of associating a real purpose and afraid of confusing them with fantasies relative to hypnosis. With the directive approaches [they used] you [the therapist] are in control. I needed to trust the person.

I went to [the] library and got a few standard texts. One of the books I read, "Hypnotic Realities" by Erickson and Rossi, that was interesting. I didn't like one passage. When he picks someone who did not want to be hypnotized and was hiding behind a pillar. That bothered me. I did like the induction. It was as I perceived. It's nontraditional and bypassed certain rationale processes. So that I felt that I would benefit from or use things in a different way. So that I was getting in a state that was not strictly me and was a process. I wanted the experience of feeling, getting into a state that I felt was hypnosis. I wanted to know that I would feel different. With others I did not feel different, but with you I did feel different. When I was talking to you, I felt changes that I had not willed myself or put myself into in a logical way. If someone had tried to do it against my will or without my knowledge, I think that is unethical. This way you know something is happening. This is the greatest way. The other ways I did not know anything was happening. When I felt...when I was in your office...I truly felt, that when you were doing your induction, and I wasn't even sure it was an induction or not, I began to feel different, so I knew something significant was taking place, and that's the truth. 'Cause something does happen—you really do feel different. You know that is different than feeling regular. It was really different. The induction itself was so different that I did not feel that I was doing anything even though I might have been. It feels as if something had occurred, that I felt that it was happening without my having to do anything.

I went to [a lay hypnotist]. Whatever he said I did; he brought me close, but nothing right was happening. [With] the other two [doctoral level psychologists] it was a light induction, stage hypnosis induction. I did not feel somatic changes. I was going along with it rather than having a part of the experience. I'm skeptical, logical, defensive. I want to know what it is precisely all about. When I find I can trust to some degree, then I can become imaginative; then my boundaries are broader than most people. Even though I am highly logical at first, I need facts [to maintain that logic]. Once this is satisfied and I have assessed the individual, I am able to say then whatever happens is pretty OK.

Weiss: What were the other therapists like?

Lois: One aroused pleasurable [almost sexual] feelings. The implication for me was very strong. Experiencing pleasurable feelings and [I could] feel this way instead of pain. Felt euphoric. He was reluctant to use pins. He did not feel there was enough time to develop it. He felt this alone could work. I felt it was him doing it rather than me doing it. I saw one [therapist] three or four times. I saw the second one one time. I saw the third once or twice.

Also, I saw a family practitioner. There was an educational presentation. Then he put me in a room with a tape. I wanted something happening that was different than every other experience I had before, and I wasn't doing it myself. In all [of the other situations] I felt relaxed, but I felt I was the author of what was happening even though I was following the suggestions. With you I felt as if I was certain that some kind of changes were taking place within me. I was just certain that it happened. All others were nice enough. I did not feel I was scared. I was going into surgery and I wanted to make sure whatever was going to happen was effective against the pain, and that is what I felt with you more than anyone else. Plus, not bleeding excessively, etc., and the healing clinic, and having a positive attitude that you incorporated in it for me, and everything worked fine as you had planned and I had hoped. I told you what I wanted and I know that you incorporated it in what you were doing or saying and I know that it happened. It did go without a hitch. It was so wonderful even my doctors were amazed. I was the talk of the hospital. I even resumed exercising a week later. I know that I healed faster. The nurses said, "You are doing so well, you had surgery this morning!" And they were amazed.

I worried about the post hypnotic suggestions, the directive stuff. It was most interesting. A couple of people tried [direct suggestions]. [I] always remembered suggestions with others. I did it only because I felt I wanted to cooperate and [I] never forgot the suggestions. I was operating on someone else's ideas, and it didn't work.

Weiss: Why Ericksonian hypnosis?

Lois: I felt that it would bypass willing cognitive, intellectual [processes. I] would be able to do it without my faculties being the sole initiating motivator. In the end, but [I] did not want to feel that I was initiating it. I wanted to feel it was a process that was occurring but not in my imagination or my will. [I] just wanted to feel more of a process independent of me even though I was involved in it. I read about Erickson—an actual method other than traditional hypnosis that was more effective—and I wanted to see if that was true for me. And it was. I heard there was no way to avoid [the] induction and [I] went in with an attitude of SHOW ME!

Weiss: What about during the surgery?

Lois: [Your] coming to hospital was real important. You really believed it and wanted to give one last reinforcement at that time [prior to surgery]. [I] did not have the faith that [I] could do it myself. I believed it was going to work and knew that I was going to be fine. I was flying. I felt really good. The doctor was interested in the way I was behaving. I was euphoric. I was not anxious. It was as if I was given Valium or something, but it was better than that. It was better than sodium pentothal. [I] felt not anxious, not scared. [I] felt happy, optimistic, everything was going to turn out fine.

Weiss: What happened before the surgery?

Lois: I was on the table [in the presurgical area] with others [who were awaiting their own surgery]. I had to sign a form or two. The anesthesiologist talked to me, explained what was happening and cooperated. I told her about [the] hypnosis. I told her more specifically: Here's the spot on my wrist. Press that. I don't want general [anesthesia] unless it's life threatening or I beg for it. I was wheeled in. Put on the operating table. Nothing frightened me. I was aware of everything going on. My pelvis was elevated off the table, etc. I felt comfortable through the whole thing. [I] remember during the operation tuning in on feathers, dogs, laughing and feeling then good. What was going on? One time, they did a local. [I] did not feel the pain of the injections [for the local] at all. After the cutting of the [superficial] cancer cells, they said, "Sure you got through that all right, but now you feel pain because the local doesn't go up that far." I actually felt pain for one moment and said "I don't have to continue feeling that pain" and that is what I did. [I] could feel it for [a] moment. [I] thought maybe he wants me to feel it for a moment. [I thought] hey, I don't want to feel. I don't want to. It is not important, [I] realized because we built that in. [I] said no more and I did not [feel it. I] felt really good. Toward the end [I] felt tired. I was glad when it was over. I could have gone on feeling no pain for as long as I wanted to do that. I knew the recovery was going to be good. [The surgical team] all looked at me. They all talked about the unusual procedure. My blood pressure was unusual…different…and my pulse was different. They said look at the smile on your face. We wish all our patients were like you down here.

Weiss: What else? What about your ability to remember or comprehend time?

Lois: I was not aware of forgetting other than the directions [that] may have been given to me. I don't think I paid attention to anything. I don't know if [the surgery] was 10 minutes or three hours. In my own mind a lot of time [passed], as time went on [I] was into my images and how I was feeling, a dog walking, a feather, or a feather walking a dog, or feeling good, giggling. [I] was singing "Nobody does it better." The smile on my face was remarked about. I said I had hypnosis. The next day I looked at my roommate and said oh I had [surgery] yesterday. She said, "You're the one that did it with hypnosis." There was very little bleeding.

Weiss: What about after the surgery?

Lois: I ate normally. I did not feel postoperative pain. I was less tired than many [people so soon after surgery]. I was talking to friends and you on the phone hours later. I was discharged 48 hours later.

Weiss: What are your recollections? Anything like a related pain since?

Lois: No pain since. No recollection of any pain since. I had a finger prick for blood tests. You know there was less anxiety.

Weiss: Have there been any generalizations to other situations since that time?

Lois: No, at first, I did for a month or two after operation, [I] felt better generally. While I was seeing you [I] felt better, a general feeling of well-being beyond on life that was occurring. It began to wear off. [I] was more energetic and optimistic, [I had] a sense of well-being and vibrancy.

Weiss: What were other people's reactions?

Lois: Everyone said you're nuts, you're crazy. The doctor said, "You showed me, I did not think it was possible, but you showed me. I believe you."

Weiss: What were the legal ramifications?

Lois: I had it put on paper what I wanted, and it was agreed upon. No anesthesia given unless it was life threatening or only if I demanded it. No tranquilizers under any consequences. I was self-responsible.

Weiss: What were the memorable aspects of the hypnotherapy?

Lois: I feel good when I'm in your presence. I felt good as you got to know me and your commitment escalated. The first induction was so important for me. I was not imaging it or willing it. It was happening. A real high point for me. The pins. No one else was willing to try. Something else about it. I felt pressure but no pain. Eye closure, it happened, without willing it or imagining it...it was happening.

One-Year Follow-up

Weiss: Were there any new learnings, understandings, or generalizations relative to what happened a year ago?

Lois: About that there are many ways to effect situations to change. I think I had a more conventional, literal approach. I think will power is a way to change. It's not necessarily the most effective. I've learned from the Ericksonian type of experience change can be effected in a light way. It doesn't have to be heavy handed and dismal, doesn't have to be so...punitive. Something that occurs because of a suggestion of a way of looking at things. Metaphor helped me use a lighter approach. Lighter is the right word. You don't always have to go in the front door. The chimney, side doors, windows—there are all sorts of ways [of] approaching [things]. It's increased my repertoire. Let's put it that way. I exercise and I see it in conjunction with [the] meditative yoga thing I've gotten into recently. I press real hard, and the harder it becomes; if I realize more and do it more easily, it just becomes more easy. I'm less militaristic with myself and more playful, another word, I think, that says it in a way.

Weiss: There is a quote of Erickson's about planting seeds and seeing what grows. Does that mean anything in relation to what happened?

Lois: Echoes and reverberations, other forms come out of that seed. Leaves stems, flowers, yes, that happens in [hypnosis], reaches other forms and aspects of your life, just as echoes and reverberations come from an original sound. Maybe the seeds planted bore fruit and flowers.

Weiss: Have there been other pain experiences? Did you use what you learned?

Lois: Yes, there was a time when I was in pain, not frequently. [Hypnosis] has helped tremendously. I remember certain images that you put in my mind. I remember recalling those specific images, and it really helped me release the pain. I remember one time I was in the car with my husband, and I don't know what happened, but I had widespread pain. It was very painful. I deliberately, I used the fingers on the wrists thing and thought of a feather walking a dog and all kind of things and was anxious and was able to get through all that and able to alleviate my pain. I thought, if it doesn't go away right now, it can later; if not, that's OK. By the time an hour went by, it went away; it happened; it was wonderful. I just simply do use it. It's a part of me. I haven't forgot it... it's a part of me.

Weiss: What is it like looking back a year later?

Lois: It was one of the best things I have ever done. Just in its efficacy it was marvelous. [I] have no regrets about it. It was [a] thorough good going experience. Maybe it was your personality, maybe it was analgesia per se, I learned to lighten up in certain ways. I think there is a connection [to the hypnosis], too.

Weiss: How is your medical condition?

Lois: I'm clean, clear. Fine. No reoccurrence. [I] had a checkup since then. Everything is OK.

Weiss: What other aspect of your life changed, if any?

Lois: I just mentioned one: lightening up. The [problems] that I went to my shrink about changed a bit. I'm serious about that. Things have gotten generally better in terms of flow. I guess, call it flow. It connects with the lightening up, I guess I'm more attracted to the positive than before. Most areas seem to be heliotropic. [I] turn toward, turning toward the light. Feathers in that thing.

Weiss: What do you mean by lightening up?

Lois: But I think a greater acceptance of things, including myself. Just degrading has become a thing that I used to be familiar with, I turn things around a little bit more easily now.

Weiss: Any concluding thoughts?

Lois: If I had another experience of surgery or involved pain, in conjunction with other methods I definitely would use Ericksonian hypnosis and the hypnotherapist I used in the first place—you!

Interpretations, Impressions and Afterthought

It seems from the above reflections and experiences that the success of the hypnoanalgesia can be traced to the fulfillment of Lois' own basic and unique needs. She needed a hypnotist who would allow her to maintain control. She needed a hypnotist who would prove that the procedure had worked. She needed someone who would allow her to be a part of the hypnotic process. She needed a hypnotist who would use her language, way of processing information, and her creative ability, and who, on a moment's notice, could utilize her needs, perceptions and desires. She needed a hypnotist who was flexible and had greater requisite variety of language, skills and expectancies. She needed a hypnotist who could create an expectancy through enchantment and intrigue. She needed a hypnotist who would come to the hospital on the day of the surgery and one who could stimulate and/or combine her own creative resources.

Lois needed a hypnotherapeutic approach that was acceptable to her personality style and psychological makeup. Thus, her experiences with the traditional, authoritarian, directive hypnotists were doomed to failure. Did her success depend upon a therapeutic approach? Perhaps, the difference is primarily that diagnostic considerations were made. This was not just another analgesia case. A script was not read. A cassette was not played. A treatment strategy and approach were created for an individual. She was an excellent YAVIS (young, attractive, verbal, intelligent, successful) and she wanted something more special than the average hypnotherapeutic subject. She was a gifted individual who would not settle for second best. She was highly and extremely responsive, but others failed because they attempted to make Lois fit an approach rather than creating an approach to fit her.

While an approach had to be painstakingly planned and structured to bring Lois into contact with prior and present meaningful life experiences and to mobilize actual or potential talent and abilities while meeting and satisfying her conscious and unconscious needs, it also had to be flexible enough to utilize her current moment. Collaboration rather than intimidation was emphasized. The approach had to allow for all possible occurrences without knowing what they were. If I had been allowed in the operating room and hypnotized the subject as I had in my office, it would have been a simple procedure. I could have monitored and corrected as needed. But in this case, Lois also had to be the therapist. Her hidden observer, which had 12 hours training in hypnotherapy and had not treated any patients, had to be not only in charge, but also competent in a possibly life-threatening situation.

I was not particularly concerned with why she wanted hypnoanalgesia, as long as she was informed of the effectiveness, risks, limitations, etc. It did not matter how her personality or psychological makeup created such a need. I did not assume there was only one way to conduct the treatment. Had I not seen her dog from my office window that day, I might never have conjured up an ambiguous function assignment. Razor blades and pins were not in my initial treatment plans. After the fifth session there were no formal treatment plans per se, just reminders on what needed to be reinforced and what was needed to deal with the unknown. My concern was to be honest, competent and, to the best of my ability, skill and knowledge, help the client achieve her goal. She was given choice, and that allowed her to fulfill her own needs.

This is what was needed; this is what was done. Lois was ready and responsive when she was ready and responsive. The Ericksonian approach expedited and facilitated that responsiveness and readiness. She was ready when she saw proof that it was going to work.

In this case the client's needs, combined with the approach taken, translated into the Ericksonian philosophy and tenets. Specifically: people make the best choice for themselves at any given moment; respect all messages from the client; teach choice, never attempt to take choice away; the resources clients need lie within their own personal history; meet the client at their model of the world; the person with the most flexibility will be the controlling element in the system (Lankton & Lankton, 1983). The Ericksonian approach paved the way, created the context, and facilitated the patient's existing abilities so that the analgesia could happen. In retrospect it was a very special and committed person, Lois, herself, who conducted the session that resulted in the ultimate success.

References

Erickson, M. H. (1966a). An introduction to the study and application of hypnosis for pain control. In J. Lassner (Ed.), *Hypnosis and psychosomatic medicine: Proceedings of the International Congress for Hypnosis and Psychosomatic Medicine.* New York: Springer-Verlag.

Erickson, M. H. (1966b). The interspersal hypnotic technique for symptom correction and pain control. *American Journal of Clinical Hypnosis, 3,* 198–209.

Erickson, M. H., & Rossi, E. L. (1979). *Hypnotherapy: An exploratory casebook.* New York: Irvington Press.

Lankton, S. R. (1984). Ericksonian approaches to psychotherapy. Seminar, Indianapolis.

Lankton, S. R., & Lankton, C. H. (1983). *The answer within: The clinical framework of Ericksonian hypnotherapy.* New York: Brunner/Mazel.

Lankton, S. R., & Lankton, C. H. (1986). *Enchantment and intervention in family therapy.* New York: Brunner/Mazel.

Leary, T. (1957). *The interpersonal diagnosis of personality.* New York: Norton.

Lustig, H. (1975). *The artistry of Milton H. Erickson, M.D., Part I and Part II.* Haverford, PA: Herbert S. Lustig, M.D. Ltd., a videotape.

Weiss, M. F. (1986). The circular metaphor model delivery pattern. Unpublished manuscript.

Hypnosis in Childbirth:
A Case Study in Anesthesia

Thomas L. South, Ph.D.

Thomas L. South, Ph.D. (Union for Experimenting Colleges and Universities) is a clinical counselor at The Counseling Center at the University of Dayton. He is founder of The Milton H. Erickson Society of Dayton and conducts workshops on clinical hypnosis.

South describes the successful use of hypnotherapy to alter the pain of childbirth and obstetrical procedures. His model uses indirect suggestion and provides an example that others can emulate. His subject had to have a caesarean delivery and a mandatory saddle-block anesthesia, which made it impossible to test the work as originally intended; however, the hypnosis resulted in a pain free reaction to all other potentially painful medical procedures.

This chapter was written as a tribute to the impact that the work of Milton H. Erickson has made in my personal and professional life. It presents a model for pain management by demonstrating the Ericksonian indirect approach to hypnosis applied to an obstetrics case. Most of the principles used are adaptations from Erickson's work. The case presented is a study of the hypnotic procedures used in a pregnancy that resulted in an unexpected caesarean birth.

The average person views pain as a distressing and intense experience over which an individual has no control, and believes that the only relief is through medication. Hypnosis can be successfully utilized for reducing or abolishing pain. The fact that the intensity of pain is altered naturally throughout the day while a person is engaged in activities enables pain to be amenable to hypnosis. It is quite difficult for the conscious mind to be aware of two different and opposing stimuli simultaneously. When an individual is consciously focusing attention, the object of interest is in the foreground while all other objects recede into the background. One definition of hypnosis states that it is a fixation of attention, and most inductions request subjects to concentrate their attention on an object or thought.

Address reprint requests to Thomas L. South, Ph.D., University of Dayton, The Counseling Center, Dayton, OH 45469.

Erickson defined hypnosis as "a communication to a person, of ideas and understandings in such a fashion that he will be most receptive to the presented ideas and thereby motivated to explore his potentials for the control and change of his psychological and physiological responses and behavior" (Erickson & Rossi, 1979, p. 94). Thus, he utilized a naturalistic approach that often consisted of a fixation of attention on the thoughts that he conveyed to patients. In the beginning of therapy, he wanted patients to be aware that they could accomplish their goals. He elicited minor changes in their attitudes by accepting the beliefs that they conveyed to him and then would subtly lead them to thinking in different ways that were more constructive to the therapeutic process.

In requesting that patients focus their attention on earlier events in their lives, he would also have them recall the physiological experiences that were associated with the events. Through his metaphors he had patients reexperience prior events and reactivated those abilities within patients that caused them to reach their goals. In the treatment of pain, Erickson taught patients to make use of previous psychoneurophysiological learnings to relieve or eliminate pain. He reactivated those memories of how the body coped in the past and how it could manage present and anticipated pain (Lankton & Lankton, 1983).

Hypnosis for pain relief varies from direct hypnotic and post-hypnotic suggestions to indirect suggestions. While the direct suggestions of traditional hypnosis are simple, unfortunately they are only effective with a small percentage of the population. Direct suggestions can alter a person's behavior as a result of compliance to the suggestion; however, the change in behavior or attitude is usually temporary because the person is only responding to a suggestion that is outside of the self. Whereas, an indirect suggestion such as, "I wonder how you are going to change your behavior," will cause inner unconscious processes of disorganizing, reorganizing, dissociating and reassociating of inner experiences to meet the requirements of the suggestion. Indirect suggestion is defined as "a suggestion that initiates an unconscious search and facilitates unconscious processes within clients so that they are usually somewhat surprised by their own response when they recognize it" (Erickson & Rossi, 1979, p. 7). Thus, if the suggestion is accepted, this new integration is a learning that the person can use in the future to gain greater insights and resolve other problems.

Indirect suggestions give stimuli to act upon, in an individual way, according to the person's experiences. This technique permits the individual to give personal meaning to the implication of the suggestion, instead of the meaning given by the therapist making direct suggestions. The indirect approach is more effective than the direct approach since it offers a wider range of choices in how to respond. All suggestions, whether direct or indirect, should be given in the best interest of the person if compliance is expected. For example: "I wonder if you will notice that pain going away now or five minutes from now?" Since the person wants the pain to subside, you are suggesting a time to the unconscious, thereby, creating an inner search. In order for suggestions to be effective, especially indirect suggestions, they must be relevant to the person as well as congruent with the person's expectations, and must be delivered with conviction.

Hypnotic anesthesia can be successfully elicited by indirect suggestion in various ways. The most straightforward approach is simply to suggest that a particular area of the body is becoming numb. However, a more indirect approach such as, "I wonder if you have already begun to notice that your hand is becoming numb," is more effective. Metaphors about natural experiences in which numbness has likely occurred, such as playing in the snow or sitting on a hand, or reminding the subject of past dental and medical anesthesias cause the unconscious to conduct an inner search to understand the implied suggestion. If the suggestion is accepted, unconscious processes will be activated to reproduce the anesthetic experience. Other techniques include dissociation, amnesia, negative hallucination, substitution, diminution, reinterpretation or reframing, and altered sensory modalities.

Hypnosis can be a valuable tool in obstetrics because of its ability to enlist as fully as possible the patient's own natural abilities and potentialities at the psychophysiological levels of functioning. It can allow the normal physiological process of pregnancy and childbirth to be a pleasant experience. Hypnosis can be used to alleviate anxiety about the anticipated pain associated with childbirth, to control weight gain, to adjust to progressive changes in the body, to relieve fatigue and other physical aches, to lessen or eliminate pain during labor, to aid the recovery process, and to cope with postpartum blues. It is not a replacement for necessary obstetrical procedures, but can be used as an adjunct to reduce the need for some traditional medical procedures. For example, it can reduce the amount of medication or chemoanesthesia normally required. Hypnotic anesthesia is also a valuable technique for problems in which drugs are not recommended. Erickson (1980a) thought that the appropriate time to employ hypnosis in obstetrics was a matter of clinical choice and judgment, but that if it were only to be used for delivery and the postpartum period, the third trimester was adequate time.

Case Report

The case that follows will demonstrate how hypnosis was successfully employed to meet the beliefs and needs of an expectant mother during the last trimester of pregnancy. It is a personal account of the techniques employed during my wife's pregnancy, delivery and recovery. I will report many of the details in order to provide a model for clinical work or for research with a larger client population.

Freda was 35 years old and in good health. Since this was her first pregnancy, she wanted to be awake during delivery without undue discomfort and wanted to breastfeed the baby. She did not want any more medication than necessary for a comfortable delivery so as not to drug the baby or herself.

Preliminary Training

The preliminary training was probably unnecessarily comprehensive since she was familiar with Erickson's reputation and had a lot of faith in his approach as well as in my ability as a hypnotherapist. She was highly motivated to prepare herself for a natural childbirth and had high expectations from reading Erickson's work. She expected the delivery to be smooth and without complications.

The first steps in Freda's training consisted of assessing the degree that she could enter trance and accept suggestions. Within 30 minutes she proved to be an excellent subject. A hand levitation and catalepsy were produced, followed by indirect suggestions for glove anesthesia, with the post-hypnotic suggestion that it was possible to sustain that anesthetic feeling after trance. Upon awakening, amnesia was created by distraction. She returned with a confused look and stated that her hand felt numb and heavy, for which she had no explanation. Another trance was induced by merely requesting that she close her eyes and relax. After her breathing changed, I induced a glove anesthesia transfer to the other hand by having her place the anesthetic hand on the other hand suggesting, "Now, let all of that numbness flow into that hand and when it has become completely numb let both hands drift down into your lap and open your eyes." She then told me that I had something to do with the numbness in her hand and was willing to experience other phenomena.

In the week that followed, Freda was taught age regression, time distortion, and negative hallucinations. Dissociation was achieved by teaching her to awaken only from the neck up and to awaken while leaving a cataleptic arm in trance.

Natural Childbirth Training

We began practicing hypnosis several times a week about the second week into the last trimester. Throughout this period, Freda was taught to experience general feelings of analgesia by utilizing the interspersal technique (Erickson, 1980b). Since we were attending Lamaze classes, I incorporated those learnings into the trancework. She learned to tense one arm while the opposite leg was relaxed and vice versa during trance until she could easily do it while awake. Next, she practiced the various breathing techniques in their sequence during trance at my signal. Freda responded well to these suggestions without any prompting or modeling on my part, as if it were second nature. This was the beginning of the nightly hypnosis sessions that lasted approximately one and one-half hours.

Caesarian Birth Training

Two weeks before the due date, the obstetrician informed us that there were complications that necessitated a caesarean section. This caught us off guard and we were very disappointed. Now Freda was dreading not being able to care for the baby as planned. The hospital policy would require a saddle-block anesthesia. But we were not easily discouraged and decided to use hypnosis to prepare for the surgery and recovery period.

The caesarean birth training began by utilizing the learnings from the preliminary training. Glove anesthesia was reinstated by indirectly suggesting dissociation through metaphors and anecdotes describing playing in the snow, the hand going to sleep, and other anesthetic experiences. After the temperature of the hands became quite cold, I suggested a glove anesthesia transfer as before, except that this time the numbness was to spread completely and thoroughly throughout her body from the top of her stomach down through her toes. This was accomplished by having the anesthetized hands lightly rub her stomach. The sensations would develop as I described and guided the numbing sensation through the various parts of her body, suggesting that there would only be a sense of touch remaining. The rubbing would cease after the entire lower extremity was anesthetized, as if she had a chemical saddle-block. Then she was reminded of pleasant events in which she had experienced time condensation (Erickson & Erickson, 1980) such as all of the things we did on vacation that passed quickly. While telling those stories, I pinched her thighs so hard I left red marks on them. Freda never so much as altered her smooth relaxed face. Pseudo-orientation-in-time (Erickson, 1980c) was then utilized to have her look forward to a successful delivery and nursing the baby. Suggestions were also given for some tolerable discomfort to remind her that she had undergone major surgery as well as suggestions for healing. Metaphors related to everyday amnesias were told before more pleasant guided imagery and awakening. This process was repeated nightly.

Amniocentesis

Five days before the caesarean birth was scheduled, we were informed that another amniocentesis was needed to check the development of the baby's lungs. The physical effects of the previous amniocentesis during the first trimester created such severe cramps that Freda was unable to work the rest of the week. Therefore, I thought that this was an excellent opportunity to test the hypnotic work.

During the three days preceding the amniocentesis, I altered the trance-work to include this procedure. After inducing the hypnotic saddle-block from the stomach to the thighs, I guided Freda through the procedure with added suggestions of seeing herself feeling quite comfortable and going to work. The morning of the amniocentesis I placed her in a deep trance and had her quickly recall the previous week's training. She was also given post-hypnotic suggestions to remain in a somnambulistic trance that would allow her to function quite normally. The procedure went smoothly. Throughout the rest of the day she felt fine, and I could not tell if she was in a waking trance. Later that evening, I awakened her. Her entire body shook convulsively and she doubled up in pain without knowing why. I mentioned that it was probably due to amniocentesis but she denied having the procedure and thought that it was scheduled for the next day. She had a complete amnesia for the entire day, and only her bloodstained undershirt and the two punctures convinced her that it had already been done. After realizing her degree of pain, I quickly placed her in a deep trance and used the previous post-hypnotic suggestions. Freda worked the rest of the week without discomfort.

Caesarean Operation

The following days were spent in preparing for surgery. During trance, Freda was reminded of our anticipated time of departure, the route to the hospital, and our estimated arrival time. She saw herself in the waiting room, filling out forms, taking last minute tests, and resting in her room anticipating the arrival of a lovely child. We also went through the caesarean section training of the previous weeks with the post-hypnotic suggestions for recovery. Before going to the hospital, Freda was placed in a deep trance and the previous week's work was rehearsed, utilizing time condensation with the embedded post-hypnotic suggestion that as she read or became aware of the interstate signs, she would gradually develop a deep somnambulistic trance that would activate all of her previous trance learnings without her conscious awareness. The learnings would remain as long as necessary to achieve the therapeutic results she needed, and could be extended one, two or three weeks, but this decision would be left entirely with her unconscious mind.

The morning of the operation, the anesthesiologist commented that my wife was the most relaxed person she had ever seen before a caesarean section. In fact, she was not satisfied with the insertion of the needle for anesthesia because it seemed too easy, and reinserted it for a saddle-block, which was normal procedure at this hospital during a caesarean birth.

I supported my wife during the operation by squeezing her hand as a distraction, and reinforcing the trance state by reframing sounds and sensations using the interspersal approach to achieve comfort and relaxation; for example, "The sensation of touch of the doctor's hands can help you continue to relax," and "I wonder how those sounds can remind you of some other pleasant experiences," and "Those pulling sensations can allow you the comfort of knowing that the baby will soon be here."

Recovery

After surgery, we were escorted to the recovery room where the surgical nurse, a former psychology student of mine, attempted to take my wife's blood pressure. She thought her instrument was malfunctioning because Freda's blood pressure was normal. The second reading with another instrument provided the same results. My former student became confused. She commented about how relaxed Freda appeared and stated, "Tom, I don't know what's going on, but you have something to do with this. Her blood pressure is normal and that's incredible, but you'll still have to spend another half-hour in the recovery room because of hospital policy."

Approximately two hours later, while in the hospital room, the chemical anesthesia wore off and Freda could move her legs. She asked me if she could take a shower to wash off the dried blood and other debris. Consent was given but with the stern warning, "You must walk very slowly by firmly placing one foot in front of the other in small steps because there will be enough discomfort to remind you that you must move slowly, and remind you that you just had major abdominal surgery." A nurse came in while she was showering and to my surprise told her, "You can't be taking a shower. Don't you know that you just had major surgery, and you're in so much pain that you can't move, let alone get out of bed and take a shower?" My somnambulistic wife informed her, "I'm taking a shower and if I'm in so much pain, why don't I feel it?" The nurse did not acknowledge this and stormed out of the room. Each day that I visited my wife and daughter, I heard the moans and screams of the other women on the floor. Freda was in good spirits, took showers and breastfed the baby. Her only complaints were that she did not know how to stop the nurses from insisting that she take pain medication.

After returning home, Freda had an amnesia for the operation and hospital stay. Weeks later, she had a fragmented memory like a dream. When asked if she wanted to recover her memory, she emphatically answered "No!" because she feared that pain would also be remembered. She was happy and amazed discovering the fragments.

Conclusion

This chapter demonstrates the successful use of hypnosis in a case of obstetrics. Erickson's indirect approach was compared with the traditional approach to hypnosis. Indirect suggestions can be used with an obstetrical patient to enlist her own natural resources to meet the needs of her situation. The necessity for caesarean delivery and the mandatory saddle-block anesthesia made it impossible to test the effect of indirect hypnotic suggestion with a natural delivery. However, the patient had a remarkably pain-free reaction to all the potentially painful medical procedures. The hypnotherapeutic methodologies employed produced a satisfactory anesthesia that was sufficient for the obstetrical procedures. The case demonstrated the therapeutic benefits that can be achieved through well-planned hypnotic training. Hopefully, the progressive stages of training outlined will serve as an effective model for obstetrical pain management.

References

Erickson, M. H. (1980a). Hypnosis in obstetrics: Utilizing experimental learning. In E. L. Rossi (Ed.), *The collected papers of Milton H. Erickson on hypnosis, Vol. IV, Innovative hypnotherapy* (pp. 224–228). New York: Irvington.

Erickson, M. H. (1980b). The interspersal hypnotic technique for symptom correction and pain control. In E. L. Rossi (Ed.), *The collected papers of Milton H. Erickson on hypnosis, Vol. IV, Innovative hypnotherapy* (pp. 262–278). New York: Irvington.

Erickson, M. H. (1980c). Facilitating objective thinking and new frames of reference with pseudo-orientation in time. In E. L. Rossi (Ed.), *The collected papers of Milton H. Erickson, Vol. IV, Innovative hypnotherapy* (pp. 424–426). New York: Irvington.

Erickson, M. H., & Erickson, E. (1980). Further considerations of time distortion: Subjective time condensation as distinct from time expansion. In E. L. Rossi (Ed.), *The collected papers of Milton H. Erickson, Vol. II, Hypnotic alteration of sensory, perceptual and psychophysiological processes* (pp. 291–298). New York: Irvington.

Erickson, M. H., & Rossi, E. L. (1979). *Hypnotherapy: An exploratory casebook*. New York: Irvington Press.

Lankton, S. R., & Lankton, C. H. (1983). *The answer within: The clinical framework of Ericksonian hypnotherapy*. New York: Brunner/Mazel.

Pain and Pleasure:
Awareness and Trust

Noelle M. Poncelet, Ph.D.

Noelle M. Poncelet, M.S.W., Ph.D. (The Fielding Institute) was Coordinator of the Chronic Pain Program, Alternative Therapies Unit at San Francisco General Hospital. She is now in private practice in San Francisco and Menlo Park, and is on the clinical faculty at the University of California at San Francisco, Department of Community Medicine, and at Stanford University, Department of Psychiatry and Behavioral Sciences. An active Ericksonian hypnosis educator, her interests center on hypnotherapy, stress management and the use of hypnosis as an adjunct for childbirth.

Poncelet describes the characteristics of people who deal successfully with chronic pain as compared with disgruntled chronic pain patients, who are usually studied. She reports that the former are health oriented, focus on life, have interests outside of pain, won't let pain stop them, use their pain for a creative purpose, trust pain, and also trust others. This study has direct application to an Ericksonian approach in which resources and assignments are part of the treatment of pain.

While some individuals suffering from chronic pain respond very rapidly to treatment, others inexplicably do not. Moreover, individuals who, during a session, experience relief from pain in trance fail to maintain and reproduce this relief on their own. These uneven results prompted a look at the effective coping strategies of well-adapted individuals, particularly in the context of their ability to experience pleasure. This chapter describes an exploratory study of chronic pain and the significance of pleasure in coping and adaptation (Poncelet, 1987) and presents clinical implications for hypnotherapy and pain management.

Background

There have been few studies of individuals who have coped successfully with pain. The few well-adapted individuals who have been systematically studied were graduates of inpatient behavioral rehabilitation programs (Painter, Seres & Newman, 1980; Roberts & Reinhardt, 1980). They

Address reprint requests to Noelle M. Poncelet, Ph.D., 271 Gabarda Way, Menlo Park, CA 94025.

were characterized by recovery from depression, decreased preoccupation with pain, increased independence from acute medical care, and return to some form of work. These programs were based on positive reinforcement of "well behaviors" such as exercises, performance of activities, and adequate pacing of work and rest (Fordyce, 1976). Rewards usually consisted of praise by others and permission for rest and leisure. The pleasure embedded in these rewards was used for its reinforcement value rather than its intrinsic value.

Cognitive approaches have focused on the negative, irrational and limiting cognitions that relate to pain, to self, to coping, and to adaptation (Turk, 1978). Cognitions related to pleasure are not emphasized. Theoreticians, on the other hand, have addressed the intrinsic value of pleasure for the survival and actualization of human beings: Lindsley (1964) developmentally, Szasz (1975) philosophically, Montagu (1978) psychologically in relation to touch, and Lowen (1970) in relation to body awareness. Lowen, in particular, stresses the importance of rhythmic full breathing for the experience of pleasure and recognizes that such breathing often prompts the release of repressed emotions which precede the experience of pleasure. The fear of the powerful emotions that accompany full breathing apparently causes individuals to constrict their breathing to avoid this affective pain. Therefore, they deny themselves the benefit of complete release and the subsequent experience of pleasure. The phenomenon is worth noting since individuals in pain tend to constrict their breathing.

Although these authors did not specifically address the issue of the role of pleasure in coping with chronic pain, an inverse correlation between depression and pleasure is well established. MacPhillamy and Lewinsohn (1974) report an increase in rate of pleasant events to correspond to a decrease in depression. This finding is particularly relevant since a relationship between depression and chronic pain has also been found (Blumer, 1985). Increase of pleasant events as a coping strategy in pain management is recommended by Bresler (1979), but he reported no empirical data to support the claim.

Two well-known professionals have combined personal experience with a scientific methodology. Norman Cousins (1976) documented his recovery from a severe collagen disease with "laughter therapy," and Milton Erickson (1980) documented the coexistence of pleasure and chronic pain. In a now classic example, Erickson told a patient suffering from phantom limb pain: "Now if you have phantom pain in a limb, you may also have phantom good feelings. And they are delightful" (Erickson & Rossi, 1979, p. 107). Indeed, Erickson's patient proceeded to demonstrate an ideosensory capacity to convert phantom limb pain into phantom limb pleasure.

This phenomenon highlights the capacity human beings have to alter reality for greater well-being in response to a suggestion that becomes congruent with personal values and belief systems.

Case Investigations

In view of the relative absence of testimony by well-adapted individuals and the paucity of information about the relationship of pleasure to chronic pain, a research study was designed to explore in-depth the role of pleasure in coping with and adapting to chronic pain. The research sample included 10 well-adapted and 10 dysfunctional individuals. The study combined objective measures and spontaneous testimony.

The criteria for eligibility were stringent. They included: medically documented muscular-skeletal pain of at least 12 months duration, some history of severe pain (6+ on visual analogue scale), light to moderate range of physical abilities, an age range of 25 to 64 years which represented independence in living and vocational status. Criteria for exclusion from the study included: an advanced life-threatening disease, other medical conditions seriously affecting functioning, an untreated affective disorder, and/or a major crisis unrelated to chronic pain in the past three months.

The well-adapted subjects consisted of vocationally active individuals who did not pursue acute medical care (surgery, hospitalization, emergency medical visit) or use of narcotics in the past six months. These subjects were recruited by word of mouth from private practitioners and outpatient clinics. The dysfunctional subjects were not working or were working in reduced, unsatisfying jobs, compared to their premorbid status. No restriction was put on their acute medical care utilization. They were recruited from two university medical centers, three private pain clinics, and private practitioners.

Information was gathered during home interviews which typically lasted four hours (including rest periods) and consisted of objective measures and open-ended questions. Taped interviews included general inquiry about pain status and current general coping strategies and specific inquiry about the subjects' awareness of pain and pleasure sensations. Body maps, the Pleasant Events Schedule (MacPhillamy & Lewinsohn, 1976, 1982), and a rated questionnaire were utilized to elicit data about frequency of experience and attitudes toward the following pleasure-related variables: variety, novelty, initiation of activity, hypnocognitive experiences, touch, rhythm, movement awareness of body comfort/pleasure, past and current family modeling, and support of pleasurable behaviors.

Findings

The two groups did not differ significantly in regard to demographic variables, experience and duration of pain, self-reported depression, or health. All members of the dysfunctional group, however, differed greatly from members of the well-adapted group in terms of physical ability even though they met the basic eligibility criterion. An immediate and important finding was that vocational status and medical care utilization were poor measures of adaptation. Both variables were influenced by situational and motivational factors. Employability, for example, was dependent on ability to sit, mobility, and employment history. High medical care utilization could be attributed to fixed medical referral routes, such as company physicians who relied on orthopedic and pharmacological interventions. In fact, several members of the dysfunctional group declared themselves satisfied with their coping strategies.

Furthermore, pleasure and its related variables did not differentiate the two groups even though they showed different degree of disability. Interestingly, no significant correlation was found, not only between pleasure as measured by the Pleasant Events Schedule (MacPhillamy & Lewinsohn, 1976, 1982) and physical ability, but also between pleasure and pain, and between pleasure and income. There was, however, a significant negative correlation in each group between pleasure and depression as measured by the Beck Depression Inventory (Beck, Rial & Rickels, 1974).

Since this investigation did not yield objective data that would help differentiate the well-adapted from the dysfunctional individual, the focus shifted to themes and patterns in the group as a whole. These themes and patterns are presented cautiously as suggestions at this exploratory stage and require further research. The first pattern was selected because of its frequency of occurrence. The others were chosen because they seemed, by their presence or absence, to shed light on the nature of stress associated with chronic pain and on the effectiveness of some coping strategies. Quotes from subjects are offered since no summary can replace or do justice to the authenticity of personal testimony.

Loss and Mourning

The theme of loss pervaded the majority of chronic pain sufferers, specifically the loss of mobility (80% of the sample) and emotional losses (75%). Emotional losses included deaths of significant persons ($n = 9$), suicide ($n = 2$), and loss of lover or dog. In addition to actual losses, many subjects had a history of child abuse or neglect ($n = 10$), marital abuse ($n = 1$), or a current discontinuation of contact with parents and/or siblings ($n = 11$).

Subjects did not usually make a connection between pain and incomplete mourning, with the following exception:

> [Since] this last episode with the back thing... I also am very aware recently that I'm not very good at mourning. I'm resisting mourning my own losses. Physical losses... When [my boyfriend] left, I never mourned that... I do have a very high pain threshold and an extreme denial ability.

Unexpectedly, unfinished mourning surfaced during pleasurable hypnocognitive activities such as daydreaming, visualizations, or spontaneous remembrance of pleasurable activities ($n = 6$). This occurrence of unfinished mourning often led to the discontinuation of these potentially helpful activities. For this sample, unresolved mourning related to physical and emotional losses appeared to increase the experience of physical pain. The mechanism of interaction between physical and emotional pain was described by one subject as muscular tension held in the body in response to negative emotions.

Body Awareness

For 65% of the sample, body awareness or lack of it emerged as an overall theme in pain management.

> People are not tuned in enough to their bodies. They think they are victims of their bodies... Your body is your friend, not your enemy. And the pain you are feeling, the tension, it is the stress you're fighting. You are fighting yourself... So I think I learned how to channel [stress] and take care of my body better.

The first theme of body awareness appeared in the role that pain, rather than pleasure, plays in calling one's attention to the body ($n = 6$). This subject has not received any pain-related psychological treatment.

> My pain lets me know I'm alive... It keeps me in my body. It makes me pay attention to myself, which I have a tendency to ignore at times, otherwise... Saying you need a break, lie down, go take a walk. BREATHE! I think that's a real big one...

Pain appears more potent than pleasure. Nowhere was this more evident than during the task of drawing pain and pleasure on two separate body maps. No participant hesitated to fill in the body map of pain, which was presented to them first. Yet, amazingly, 65% were hesitant about identifying areas of comfort and pleasure in the same body, and 75% either checked what did not hurt or said that they did not pay attention to places that did not hurt. Most left out large areas of their body—trunk or limbs, front or back—that were neither painful, comfortable, nor pleasurable, but simply out of their awareness. Interestingly, half the sample had at least some partial overlap between areas of pain and comfort/pleasure.

The second theme is that body awareness was found to play a positive and pleasurable role in increasing the effectiveness of strategies used to deal with chronic pain. These strategies included taking charge of one's body ($n = 6$), deep breathing ($n = 4$), proprioceptive activities that emphasized awareness of minimal harmonious movements rather than performance and endurance ($n = 10$), and hypnocognitive experiences ($n = 7$).

> I've learned how to use my breath as a tool to focus energy... to appreciate how much movement is related to breath... sort of seeing the ways the body has of letting go and then using that to move rather than trying to force things in an active mode... Appreciation for using sound and coordinating sound and movement together and making sounds myself. That's been real interesting. And becoming sensitive to the small movements that the body can make... and making that a challenge. The physical therapy I had before, the reason I was so frustrated, it was that it was just strengthening. I mean 10 leg lifts. It was boring and it was so limited. Now, in a way I'm just getting to the point where I can really commit myself to deal with strengthening exercises... It's hard to explain but it [Aston Patterning] has been very nurturing and restoring so that now somehow I can do my strengthening exercises and not feel like it's punishment.

Many subjects ($n = 16$) used spontaneously devised visualizations or fantasy to relax their body and bring them comfort and pleasure. An interesting distinction began to emerge because of the use by six participants of clearly active pleasurable hypnocognitive experiences, in contrast with tranquil passive visualizations such as being in nature. These active hypnocognitive activities consisted of visualizing one's body *doing* physical activities one could not experience at that moment or ever. An important need may thus be fulfilled for some individuals, as was demonstrated by one subject who denied herself such active daydreaming because it triggered unresolved mourning, and yet, who experienced herself in dreams full of fast action. The following quote conveys the sensorial awareness and the usefulness of spontaneous daytime dissociation in time and space.

> The way I am remembering past pleasure is very physical... There was a lake I used to swim in when I was a child, and I sometimes can smell the water... and I can feel it. It was a very rocky beach and it

was a rocky approach getting in, and I can actually feel those sharp rocks on the way to this ultimate pleasure, which was swimming in this gorgeous, beautiful lake. I can smell the pine trees that were near the shore and were a part of the whole experience of being in this particular lake... It [the imagery] flashes in and out, I'd have to say at least three, four or five times a day, and it's not really on a very conscious level. It's just sort of there underneath my preparations to go to work. It's sort of a friend, it's a companion kind of to another activity which is on top of it.

The third theme that emerged is an effective cognitive process described by the participants ($n = 8$) who were most satisfied with their adaptation. This cognitive process consists of volitional focus of attention and awareness in ways described as 1) going into the pain no matter how severe as a voluntary attentional process, 2) dealing with this pain by using a variety of idiosyncratic strategies, 3) then taking the pain along by allowing it to remain present to whatever degree and making no effort to distract oneself from it, and 4) actively focusing on a pleasurable activity in the moment.

Going into the pain, paradoxically, gave control. A 63-year-old woman with rather severe arthritis in her feet, who had never received psychological treatment for her pain, described the process first cognitively, then behaviorally:

> Yeah, it [pain] is a challenge... I think I handle the pain, because I go into it... I don't dwell on it. I just go along as if it wasn't there... It isn't denying it. It's just letting it be a part of you, and once it's a part of you, the whole of you, then it loses its importance... I think that pain increases with tension or with fighting it... if you're relaxed and go into it, then it just dissolves because your body is more relaxed... Just let my body flow... Because I don't feel like I'm a victim. I won't let it make me a victim. If my attitude is such that I'm in charge, then it can't affect my life. I go with it, I recognize it, I'll walk along with it but I'm not going to let it stand in my way.

> I walk on my toes if it's painful just to go into the pain. I massage or my husband massages them. I have a chiropractor work with me. I keep on doing everything so that it doesn't get any worse. I visualize myself continuing on with everything...I feel it [pain] is getting even better.

Interestingly, pain control was achieved whether participants treated the pain as friend or as enemy. The "strugglers," however, tended to complain more of fatigue than the others.

[My pain] responds well to being *attacked* through visualization and the relaxation.... I regularly demonstrate [that I am more powerful than it is] by putting it in a pen... A *wild animal in a crate*... I'm real successful but I'm not functional... I can't put it in a cage and talk to you or take a walk or go swimming... Someday I'll be able to do that.

The experience of a subject who remarkably eliminated an injury-related back pain of six years duration deserves mention. She started with a fighting approach and changed to a positive approach, which she describes in terms of feminine and masculine processes. One night of extreme pain, she lay on the floor:

I chose to just be directly with the pain... I connected totally with the pain in that moment... and I realized that there was something [anger and mourning] in me that was still tied to the accident... It literally could not be anymore, otherwise I'd end up crippled for the rest of my life. And I did no conscious act of severing the cord, except when I saw it, it severed.

It was a pure, clean focus in there, with no condemnation, no criticism, no rejection, nothing... [Being receptive to pain is] like coming into a very feminine side of myself and... in order to move through it [sever the connection between the emotional and physical pain], there needs to come a penetration of the spirit of the masculine that will focus on an action that will move you through and out of, but broaden at the same time, as a human being.

The bridges between pain and pleasure appear to be focusing attention and control. Focusing attention is active rather than reactive. Control is the decision to voluntarily open to pain and to choose to enjoy the moment. Pleasure occurs in the awareness of the moment ($n = 10$).

It's up to me to enjoy things. I can be bored or I can choose not to be bored... I can choose to be depressed [by my pain], or I can choose to get up and go out the door and walk and not be depressed...

I don't know where the idea comes to do something pleasurable. I guess I'm always open. I'm always thinking about what I can do that I can enjoy. I try to find some pleasure out of the moment.

He's never stopped being turned on to me physically... The pleasure of making love just makes you forget the pain. It dulls. It just transcends it, and it's very energizing and it makes you feel wonderful and powerful, and to continue to feel beautiful, I guess attractive, whatever. It makes you want to get better... The best possible escape. It's better than drugs.

Trust

Trust, partial trust, or absence of trust appears to be the integrative element, the systemic glue, that permeates the previously discussed themes and contributes to adaptation to chronic pain. In this context, trust refers to a dynamic interaction of factors: confidence, competence, positive regard and openness. It is an action, a process rather than a trait. Trust is an act of confidence in one's competence, in one's ability to use personal resources as well as to tap others' resources, such as family members and health care professionals, in coping with life experiences. Trust is the confidence that it is safe and desirable to be inside one's body, to keep one's awareness inside the body, to have an acceptance of pain and pleasure as an opportunity to grow. There is a willingness to be fully attentive to, and conscious of sensorial, affective and cognitive experiences, with the expectation of a positive outcome. In a receptive sense, the interaction of openness with trust means being available to the unknown and to change; in an expressive sense, it is to be in charge. Trust is to enter the grief embedded in pain with positive regard and confidence that the insult, be it temporary or partial loss of physical well-being, abandonment or abuse, does not invalidate or diminish the self but strengthens it. Assuming this pain, trust is to enter pleasure and experience it as nourishment rather than simply as a distraction and relief from pain.

A subject describes the coping process for chronic pain, and then the significance of pleasure:

> To let go... of past learning, suspicion. To trust, I think. To become like a child, I think, sort of willing to start all over again, to literally learn how to walk.

> The surgery, although it rendered me unable to use my arms, also... was a vehicle for incredible growth for me... and I see the pain is a continuation of that, an opportunity to grow... It sort of began an internal journey that I had neglected during all these many years... It started, I think, with appreciating the fact that other people could actually help me... Accepting that, somehow I acknowledged that I could love myself, that I could help myself, and that I could meet my own needs...

Pleasure is wonderful. It is why we are alive, I think… I enjoy it more
[since I've been in pain]… It's just that pleasure is enhanced and I
find pleasure in more places than I used to… Probably, [it's because]
I'm more aware of my own mortality, perhaps, and that each day
we're either living or we're dying. It's just a matter of what flip of the
coin. If you decide for living and until these last moments when
you're dying, it just seems to me valuable to learn as much and be as
much a part of the experience of life as I can be.

A Model

Burt (1984) provocatively suggests that what an individual *presupposes*
about the nature of health and the human condition in general plays a
major role in dysfunction and quality of life. The presupposition underlying the design of this study was that accomplishment and performance
(i.e., work and health) were means to achieve quality of life. Instead, the
results of this study suggest that what is centrally important is not performance but awareness of self-in-body (as a means), and the desire to
learn more about self (as a motivational force). In this context, pain may be
reframed as a friend, as an opportunity to learn more about the body at
rest and in movement, and to learn more about and integrate apparent
polarities: pain and pleasure, being and doing, body and mind/spirit.
When awareness of self-in-body is allowed to lead to learning, and learning leads to growth, pain and pleasure are viewed as intrinsic to learning
about self. To be healthy is valued but no longer essential.

In this study participants illustrated the ups and downs of living with
chronic pain. Many had difficulty living consciously in their bodies. A
reason for this reluctance to live consciously in one's body may be fear of
the dangers inherent in the human condition, and ultimately fear of death.
What makes awareness not only bearable but also inspiring as a learning
experience is trust, as the dynamic interaction of confidence, competence,
positive regard and openness. Trust, in effect, is a presupposition similar to
a positive presupposition proposed by Burt (1984): that humans have the
capacity to co-create the fateful events that shape their lives.

In this study, trust translated into a willingness 1) to take charge by
using both personal and external resources, 2) to experience pain as a
meaningful activity, 3) to pursue and enjoy pleasurable experiences, 4) to
gain from treatments that enhance body and movement awareness, and
5) to use spontaneously devised hypnocognitive activities that access
body memories of comfort and pleasure in rest and in movement. Trust
permits alignment between awareness of self in time and in space. Thus,
when the body in pain reactivates past physical and/or emotional pain, in

a trusting awareness this experience of pain is met not with panic or rejection but with openness and acceptance. At the body level, trust manifests itself by breathing fully. Cognitively, it translates into positive visions for the future.

Some participants expressed unwillingness to risk being aware of the body in pain, be it physical and/or emotional, or of pleasure in self or in relationships. Mistrust translated into fear and into muscular tension. It resulted in avoidance of pleasurable daydreaming that spontaneously evoked feelings of loss and grief, and in termination of a physical therapy regimen experienced as punishment or torture.

In this circular interactive model of coping with chronic pain, mistrust in one area—be it pain, pleasure, body, self, or relationships—may lead to an avoidance of awareness in that area and to a fear of learning, exploring and discovering in that area and any other connected area. Thus, ultimately, any mistrust will affect general adaptation to chronic pain in a way specific for each individual.

The drive to learn about self that emerges in the formulation of this model can be found in the testimonies of several participants. They were among the most satisfied, as well as the ones who volunteered in the hope that they might learn something by participating in the study. Indeed, Erickson (1958), an individual suffering from chronic pain most of his life, based his hypnotic inductions for pain control on the ever-present motivation to learn and discover.

This proposed model, surprisingly, turns out to be closer to Eastern philosophies that emphasize "being" and awareness (Levine, 1982) rather than to traditional Western values that emphasize "doing" and performance. Yet it is parallel and complementary to Bandura's (1977) self-efficacy model. Both models focus on competence, and recognize the powerful modeling effect of significant others on learning. According to Bandura, "an efficacy expectation is the conviction that one can successfully execute the behavior required to produce the outcomes" (p. 193). Trust as defined in this study is the conviction that one can, in a satisfying manner, learn from being aware of the experience before moving into action. This study suggests that for chronic pain, this process of awareness may be an important step that will potentiate successful performance of coping strategies, especially when successful performance does not prevent the problem (pain) from recurring. Satisfaction may be as dependent upon awareness of meaningful learning about self-in-body as on successful performance. The two cognitive models, far from being mutually exclusive, enhance each other, as "doing" cannot exist without "being."

This model may help resolve a problem that has been troublesome from the start of this study: how to define satisfaction regarding coping with and adapting to chronic pain. Satisfaction apparently needs to be examined as a function of underlying presuppositions that define, for each individual, external variables, rather than, as this study attempted to do, externally imposed variables of vocational status and medical care utilization.

Clinical Implications

This model has clinical implications for psychotherapy and hypnotherapy at the assessment and treatment levels.

Assessment

The best assessments are those that follow the patient's internal experience and start with the pain experience. Assessment should include the history of current pain and of early childhood and current physical, sexual, and emotional abuse or neglect, and unmourned or incompletely mourned losses. Absence of current contact with family of origin is also a significant indicator of trouble.

During the assessment process, carefully identify areas of functioning and coping strategies that have been used. In particular, be aware of the beneficial and detrimental consequences of spontaneous hypnocognitive activities which produce dissociation. On the negative side, dissociation may maintain awareness outside the body. It may also bring up unresolved grief which, if it is met with resistance, may result in muscular tension, impede a smooth transition between the trance state immobility and motion in the awakening state, and translate in jerky, painful movements. On the positive side, dissociation to active pleasant physical experiences may enhance body awareness and offer an opportunity for active rehearsing of flowing movement in preparation for physical activities in the alert state. Therefore, note the circumstances that have accompanied partial successes or failures.

Rarely does an individual with chronic pain function poorly in all areas of life. The role of pleasure in areas of positive functioning as well as prior to pain onset needs to be assessed and its relationship to the maintenance of depression established. The map of comfort/pleasure offers an easy way to explore the degree of sensorial pleasure awareness present in an individual suffering from chronic pain. The map may help define barriers to positive physical awareness. Like the Pleasant Events Schedule, it is a teaching tool that conveys the value and importance given to pleasure by the clinical team. The Pleasant Events Schedule is both informational (rate of pleasure reinforcement) and educational (a reminder of how much pleasure there is) and can help patients to reinstate pleasure behaviorally in their everyday lives. Simple questions such as "What do you do for fun?" and "What did you use to do for fun?" offer valuable information for later interventions.

A surprisingly effective way of indirectly checking for presuppositions is to look for the presence of positive visions of the future. This offers an opportunity to identify areas of trust or fear related to self, body, pain, pleasure, relationships, and the health care system. Patients will indicate through their language whether they are in charge by the use of "I" statements, or whether they are victims of circumstances happening to them. Additionally, a line of openly existential questions often brings relief and release of concern even when there is initial surprise and discomfort. When alignment of body, mind, and spirit is examined, many patients are found to be de-spirited, without an inspiring vision that makes life worth living, and often they are not even aware of this lack. Appropriate questions include: "What is inspiring to you about living even though you are in pain?" "What makes life worth living?" "What does death mean to you?" "If it was up to you, what would death mean to you?" and "If you had three wishes, what would you want to experience?"

Physical therapy has a crucial role to play in gently developing or enhancing comfortable awareness of harmonious movement and gentle touch. This awareness is a necessary step in regaining trust in a painful body and in fostering motivation for exercise. If the patient is involved in a performance and endurance-oriented program, encourage involvement in programs that foster the importance of being fully aware of self-in-body in pain as well as in pleasure. Such programs might include the Feldenkrais Awareness through Movement Reeducation, Aston Patterning, Alexander Method, or other forms of therapeutic massages.

Treatment

As Erickson taught and practiced, and as well-adapted subjects in this study testified, the following processes are important in pain reduction: *pace* the pain experience and be willing to invite the patient initially to *amplify* the pain at the beginning of trance, instead of attempting distraction from pain. Amplify the sensations of pain and the emotions of grief, frustration, and fear attached to this pain. Your willingness to meet patients in their internal subjective experience conveys your trust in the integrity of the body in pain and in the embedded opportunity for further learning and growth. You are modeling that pain can be met with curiosity as a learning opportunity rather than as threat and punishment. The basic question is not how individuals suffering from chronic pain can be what they no longer are, but how can they be in their own eyes, the very best individuals with chronic pain.

Age regression is useful in two ways, and the patient's process will determine which one to use. The first goal is to revisit events of physical and emotional pain particularly during an abusive childhood. Using Erickson's (1980b) February Man approach or the following approach, correct these events and establish a new link between the prior event and the present experience.

Freeing Pain from the Past
(after establishing a light to moderate trance)

Imagine a thread linking all the experiences you have had in your life with emotional and physical pain and suffering (name them as you know of them)... See the color of this thread linking each event and these events sprouting as balloons of different colors and dimensions and designs on the map of your life. Feel the texture of this thread as you hear the balloons bouncing in the wind... Now bring your attention to each balloon and as you step inside, one last time let the experience tell you fully how it contributed to who you have become, what you learned from that pain that was helpful. See and feel the scar it has left on you and appreciate the distinctive character it gives to your being as it heals more and more, leaving eventually the tiniest of marks. Honor all the feelings you are experiencing, all the thoughts and the sensations without judgment, without blame and release them in the atmosphere... When you feel satisfied that there is no more to learn about it at this time, when you are ready, take a pair of scissors and cut the thread so that the balloon can now lift and join all the balloons that ever lifted, leaving behind the scar to honor and appreciate. Allow yourself to proceed with each balloon. Letting go of the little ones first or the big ones, whichever you prefer. If you get to one that you absolutely cannot let go of, accept yourself without judgement, without blame. There is still something there to learn.

Focus now again on your current sensation of discomfort and enjoy it in its new space, without the clutter of all the other hidden ones. Continue to breathe space in and around it...

(Continue on with other messages or terminate with suggestions for self-appreciation.)

The second goal of an age regression trance is to access prior experiences of active pleasure, such as dancing, playing childhood games, swimming, hiking, engaging in sports, or running, in order to establish a counterrhythmic experience to the pain. This trance needs to be a revivification, a stepping-into the experience, with a detailed focus on exquisite body sensations, pleasurable feelings, and self-appreciation. Very carefully invite the patient to carry the flowing feelings experienced in the trance into the movements needed to reorient and to move at the end of the trance.

Dissociations in time and space appear ideally suited because they offer a focus on body awareness and on positive and pleasurable sensorial imagery in its proprioceptive and kinesthetic forms. Clinicians can easily capitalize on patients' spontaneous use of daydreaming and visualizations by encouraging active daydreaming immediately preceding physical activities.

Create *metaphors* for self-empowerment with the following embedded messages: I have internal resources; I hire my own helpers. In an extended trance, invite patients to discover their inner advisor (Lankton & Lankton, 1983), their power animals, their spirit helpers. Both Bresler (1979) in the Western tradition and Harner (1980) in the Shamanistic tradition provide examples of this powerful self-healing experience.

Future orientation in time offers an opportunity for the patient to cocreate and rehearse the future in response to the crucial question: "What do I want rather than what do I deserve or can expect? If it is up to me, if there are no strings attached, what do I really want?" The task is to help the individual develop, in increasingly finer detail, what he or she desires, to be clear that this vision is deserved, and to be willing to assume its consequences. This process may require more than one session. Clinically, most often a change is noticed after the patient has owned and released a vision, thus trusting its capacity to manifest itself.

Above all, hypnosis can be used to assist the patient to *shift attention* from pain to pleasure. The effectiveness of this trance does not depend on severity of pain; it depends essentially on timing, i.e., on the individual's readiness to receive the following messages after the groundwork has been laid.

Opening to Pain and Pleasure

Make yourself as comfortable as you can right now… knowing that you can readjust your body for increasing comfort any time you need to do so… As you become aware of your breathing, know that you can let my words envelop you with comfort so you can rest from all the effort that you have been devoting to taking care of yourself… And I am going to focus on suffering because you are learning a lot about suffering as you experience this pain and discomfort in your back…

As you breathe in and out, I would like to ask you to go deeper and deeper inside your body. As you breathe in, allow yourself, if you wish, to breathe space *around* the areas of discomfort in your back... With each breath, allow the parts of you that surround the pain to gently soften and open and relax around this pain so that it can begin to have the space necessary to move. Open this area as you open a fist that has been clutching onto something... That's right... Begin to give a chance to this pain to go somewhere... You're doing fine... The adjacent areas becoming softer and softer with each breath... There is no need to hurry. Simply allow your breath to do the work. Your body knows how to gently and safely open to your breath...

Now allow yourself to focus on the area of most pain and discomfort, and with this next breath, breathe space *inside* your pain. With this breath enter this pain as if you are an explorer on a journey. Notice all the details and nuances, the colors, shapes, textures, the rhythm, the taste and smell of this pain. See images embedded inside this pain. Allow yourself the relief of suspending judgment and blame on yourself, on your thoughts, your feelings, your sensations... Simply notice, learn and release what you are experiencing without judgment, without blame... And gently, without effort, allow your unconscious to bring up to you the valuable lessons embedded in your experience so that you can retain the lessons and release that which is no longer needed... You're doing fine.

And as you continue to breathe in space into this pain, the pain now can begin to gently dissolve, hardly noticeable at first... The more gently and fully you breathe, the more this pain dissolves into this newly found space. And you can do this for the other areas of pain, entering them, knowing them, learning from them about suffering and releasing them as the pain begins to dissolve more and more into the newly found space... That's right.

Now, when you're ready and not before, allow yourself to shift your focus to areas nearby which you will be pleasantly surprised to notice are very comfortable, and gently breathe space around and into this area so that it too can move and become even more comfortable and pleasurable than it already is... That's right... Now if you find your attention drifting back to the areas of discomfort and pain, that's all right too. Honor your attention and gently bring it back to the areas of comfort and pleasure, noticing a network linking all these pleasurable cells in your body. As you enter one of them, notice all the details and nuances, colors, shapes, textures and rhythm, learn the messages deeply embedded there, and release. No judgment, no blame. Accepting and enjoying. Accepting and enjoying.

NOW, I'd like to invite you to travel to this one tiny point within yourself that is the essence of who you are—most wise, most loving, most competent. It may be located somewhere behind your heart, maybe somewhere else. You'll know. With this next gentle breath, step into it. It's the hologram of who you've always been, will always be—most loving, most wise, most competent. As you safely nest and rest inside, let your essence nurture and take care of you, refueling you with energy, with hope and with confidence as you open more and more. And know yourself being more than pain, more than pleasure, beyond pain and pleasure... From this place of tranquility and peace, see the rhythms of pain and the rhythms of comfort and pleasure come together in a dance, their rhythms aligning in a most harmonious and mutually satisfying flow where they remain separate and yet become one in this dance where the dancer, the danced, and the dance are one. Experience the beauty of this dance deeply and so comfortably as your ears get filled with the accompanying music...

And you discover more and more now that the pain can dissolve and leave or comfortably recede far in the background... that, if new pain comes in later, it will teach you and leave or comfortably recede far in the background. And the comfort can come in and leave, making room for more comfort to come in and also be released. And thus you can continue to learn and grow and expand and become more who you truly are.

Now without actually moving, imagine yourself getting out of this chair and moving around comfortably as you will do shortly... That's right... and when you're ready, allow yourself to become alert and oriented to this room, and those parts of you that need it can comfortably remain in a trance as you move on to your next activity feeling relaxed, refreshed, and renewed with energy, appreciating deeply who you and your body are. Thank you.

Conclusion

The coexistence of pain and pleasure, regardless of the severity of pain or level of disability, appears to be facilitated by a willingness to be aware of self-in-body and to trust, as this exploratory study suggests. More clinical observations and research are needed, and the testimonies of many more well-adapted individuals would be invaluable.

The clinical suggestions that emerged from this study, as well as from many years of clinical experience with pain patients, apply particularly to individuals suffering from chronic muscular-skeletal pain. Far from being exhaustive, they overlap with or are complementary to the many powerful techniques, such as analgesia, anesthesia, amnesia, dissociation, interspersal suggestions, displacement, replacement, substitution and catalepsy that were described by Erickson (1980a).

To help human beings open fully in awareness and trust to their experience of pain and pleasure is one of the most formidable and most rewarding challenges for the clinician. It is one where patient and clinician lead each other in constant exploration of the unknown.

References

Bandura, A. (1977). Self-efficacy: Toward a unifying theory of behavioral change. *Psychological Review, 84*, 191–215.

Beck, A. T., Rial, W. Y., & Rickels, K. (1974). Short form of Depression Inventory: Cross validation. *Psychological Reports, 34*, 1184–1186.

Blumer, D. (1985). Chronic pain and depression: The pain-prone disorder. In C. Van Dycke, L. Temoshok, & L. S. Zegans (Eds.), *Emotions, in health and illness: Applications to clinical practice*. New York: Grune & Stratton.

Bresler, D. E. (1979). *Free yourself from pain*. New York: Simon & Schuster.

Burt, J. (1984). Metahealth: A challenge for the future. In J. D. Matarazzo, J. A. Herd, N. E. Miller, & S. M. Weiss (Eds.), *Behavioral health* (pp. 1239–1245). New York: Wiley.

Cousins, N. (1976). Anatomy of an illness (as perceived by the patient). *New England Journal of Medicine, 295*, 1458–1463.

Erickson, M. H. (1958). Pediatric hypnotherapy. *American Journal of Clinical Hypnosis, 1*, 25–29.

Erickson, M. H. (1980a). Hypnotherapeutic approaches to pain. In E. L. Rossi (Ed.), *Collected papers of Milton H. Erickson on hypnosis* (Vol. 4, pp. 235–236). New York: Irvington.

Erickson, M. H. (1980b). The February man: Facilitating new identity in hypnotherapy. In E. L. Rossi (Ed.), *Collected papers of Milton H. Erickson on hypnosis* (Vol. 4, pp. 525–542). New York: Irvington.

Erickson, M. H., & Rossi, E. (1979). *Hypnotherapy: An exploratory casebook*. New York: Irvington.

Fordyce, W. E. (1976). *Behavioral methods for chronic pain and illness*. St. Louis: C. V. Mosby.

Harner, M. (1980). *The way of the shaman*. New York: Harper & Row.

Lankton, S., & Lankton, C. (1983). *The answer within*. New York: Brunner/Mazel.

Levine, S. (1982). *Who dies?* Garden City, NY: Anchor Books.

Lindsley, D. B. (1964). The ontogeny of pleasure: Neural and behavioral development. In R. Heath (Ed.), *The role of pleasure in behavior* (pp. 3–22). New York: Harper & Row.

Lowen, A. (1970). *Pleasure: A creative approach to life*. New York: Coward-McCann.

MacPhillamy, D. J., & Lewinsohn, P. M. (1974). Depression as a function of levels of desired and obtained pleasure. *Journal of Abnormal Psychology, 83*, 651–657.

MacPhillamy, D. J., & Lewinsohn, P. M. (1976). *Manual for the pleasant events schedule*. Unpublished manuscript, University of Oregon (Mimeo).

MacPhillamy, D. J., & Lewinsohn, P. M. (1982). The pleasant event schedule:

Studies on reliability, validity, and scale intercorrelation. *Journal of Consulting and Clinical Psychology, 50*, 363–380.

Montagu, A. (1978). *Touching: The human significance of the skin* (2nd ed.). New York: Harper & Row.

Poncelet, N. M. (1987). *Chronic pain and the significance of pleasure in coping and adaptation.* Unpublished dissertation. Ann Arbor, MI: University Microfilms International.

Painter, J. R., Seres, J. L., & Newman, R. I. (1980). Assessing benefits of pain center: Why some people regress. *Pain, 8*, 101–113.

Roberts, A. H., & Reinhardt, L. (1980). The behavioral management of chronic pain: Long-term follow-up with comparison groups. *Pain, 8*, 151–162.

Szasz, T. S. (1975). *Pain and pleasure: A study of bodily feelings* (2nd ed.). New York: Basic Books.

Turk, D. C. (1978). Cognitive-behavioral techniques in the management of pain. In J. P. Foreyt & D. J. Rathjen (Eds.), *Cognitive behavior therapy: Research and application.* New York: Plenum.

Presenting Ideas to Phobics

John A. Moran, Ph.D.

John A. Moran, Ph.D. (University of Maryland) is in independent practice in Scottsdale, Arizona. He served as Associate Director of The Milton H. Erickson Foundation and is president of the Phobia Society of Arizona.

Moran gives us five principles for packaging therapeutic ideas to clients with phobias and illustrates them with several cases from his own work and several lesser known cases from Erickson.

Milton Erickson taught that therapy consists of presenting ideas in ways that the individual can use them (Zeig, 1985a). Most ideas presented by the therapist are already known by the client (Haley, 1976). One therapeutic goal, then, is to present these known ideas in ways that will stimulate change within the client.

This chapter conveys how the principles and practices of the Ericksonian approach to therapy guide the treatment of phobias. It is organized into five sections, with each section headed by a principle of the Ericksonian approach (Zeig, 1985a, 1985b). Each principle is discussed in relation to the problem of phobias. The five principles are:

1. Meet the individual at his or her level of influence.
2. Identify unaccessed strengths of the individual and connect them to the problem.
3. Get the individual to do something.
4. Utilize confusion and illogic to disrupt maladaptive sets.
5. Use social systems.

Principle 1: Meet the Individual at His or Her Level of Influence

A panic attack is a conversion experience: At one moment the person is not phobic and at the next moment he or she is. Only a few panic attacks are needed for an individual to develop an intense preoccupation with physical

Address reprint requests to John A. Moran, Ph.D., Psychological Counseling Services, Ltd., 3337 N. Miller Rd., Suite 105, Scottsdale, AZ 85251.

functioning. Such preoccupation can develop without a panic attack as exemplified by a homosexual man who was in treatment for generalized anxiety. He tested positive for having been exposed to the AIDS virus. The physician explained the risks of the patient's condition as they were known at that time. In response to questions by the patient, the physician said that an early warning sign of progression of the disease would be vertigo or slight feelings of dizziness. Consequently, the patient detected symptoms of dizziness getting out of bed in the morning, climbing stairs, going in and out of the heat in Phoenix, in cars that were accelerating and decelerating, in elevators, on stairways, and so forth. To generalize from this case to therapeutic technique: To meet phobics at their level of influence, the therapist needs to attend to their preoccupation with physical functioning and comfort.

People with phobias are a diverse group, but usually phobics have another preoccupation—preoccupation with the logical. Nearly all therapists have been exposed to the curvilinear relationship between anxiety and performance: After a point, increased anxiety compromises intellectual and behavioral competence. Phobics, at the moment of most intense anxiety, are gripped by overwhelming irrational fear. They often believe they are going to die or go crazy. Reflexively, phobics seize logic with both fists as an antidote to the irrational. It is not unusual for phobics to have an extensive library about phobias which includes magazine and newspaper articles, tapes of television programs, and tapes purchased through mail order houses to help them relax or otherwise deal with the phobia. The therapist can use this preoccupation with the logical and with physical comfort as a hidden resource for treatment (Zeig, 1985a).

Principle 2: Identify Unaccessed Strengths in the Individual and Connect Them to the Problem

The solution to their problem most phobics use is avoidance. When avoidance is no longer feasible, medication is often used. More enduring, less intrusive solutions are available through therapy using the psychological operations of guided attention, dissociation, and amnesia. The therapy experience begins with a diagnostic assessment. With phobias the initial process is vitally important to the success of the therapy. Giving a diagnosis is the traditional way of using logic to approach a problem. The diagnosis guides attention toward solution. An Ericksonian technique is to present the diagnosis so that it empowers the individual. Even though most phobics know they have phobias, they still want to know "What is wrong with me that I have this problem?" This question offers a prime opportunity to present a meaningful idea.

For example, a 33-year-old woman began to experience panic attacks about one year after she stopped using heroin. Despite her problem with drugs, she had graduated from college. At the time she was treated, she was married and working as a legal assistant. She experienced panic attacks when driving alone, in crowds, and sometimes when she and her husband discussed their sex problems. As the initial session drew to a close, she was told:

> You are a resourceful person whose body has signaled overload even though your capacities have not been fully taxed. Your problem is threat-sensitivity and the way you respond to threat.
>
> You respond to threat with anxiety. The anxiety gets worse if you run away from the threat. On the other hand, if you fight the threat, you further exhaust yourself, making yourself more threat-sensitive.
>
> I have an intervention for you that will work. The intervention is devilishly simple, but hard to do. It will not work unless you truly appreciate how threat-sensitive you are and how you have no other recourse but this intervention. So, before I give you the intervention I want you to take a week to consider how often you are threatened and how helpless you are in responding to threat.

The next session the woman returned with an elaborated list of events that caused her stress. She was told:

> Stress is just a polite word for threat. I don't think you yet comprehend the amount of threat you encounter. Threat comes as fast as words, feelings, and ideas—as fast as the speed of light. You've told me you were threatened by panic, by being away from other people, by thinking you won't get your work done, by being in conflict with your husband. You haven't mentioned being threatened by others' disappointment in you, being afraid of criticism by others, believing you are inferior to others, being embarrassed, being frustrated, being insulted, thinking of past misdeeds, of possible future problems, of objects you can't afford to purchase, of social performance demands, by a feeling of fatigue or boredom, by the impulse to get angry or overeat, or an unkempt household.

For the next half-hour the session focused on examining the types, number, and intensity of the threats to which she was exposed. After this she was given a long, detailed explanation about the biochemistry of the fight/flight syndrome. Toward the end of the session she was told the intervention was to help her to become an expert in blocking threat. She was then told the following story:

> Once, when a disciple came to a master to be disciplined in the art of fencing, the master, who was in retirement in his mountain hut, agreed to undertake the task. The pupil was made to help him gather wood for kindling, draw water from the nearby spring, split wood, make the fire, cook rice, sweep the rooms and the garden, and generally look after his household affairs. There was no regular or technical teaching in the art. After some time the young man became dissatisfied, for he had not come to work as a servant to the old gentleman, but to learn the art of swordsmanship. So one day he approached the master and asked him to teach him. The master agreed. The result was that the young man could not do any piece of work with a feeling of safety. When he began to cook rice early in the morning, the master would appear and strike him from behind with a stick. When he was in the midst of his sweeping, he would feel the same blow from somewhere, from an unknown direction. He had no peace of mind, he had to be always on the lookout for the master's attack. Some years passed before he could successfully dodge the blow from whatever source it might come. But the master was not satisfied with him yet. One day the disciple found the master cooking his own vegetables over an open fire. He took it into his head to avail himself of this opportunity. Taking up his big stick, he let it fall over the head of the master who was then stooping over the cooking pan to stir its contents. The pupil's stick was caught by the master with the cover of the pan. This opened the pupil's mind to the secret of the art. He then truly appreciated for the first time the unparalleled kindness of the master (Herrigel, 1971, pp. 81–82).

After the story the woman was asked to continue, until the next appointment, to observe threat sensitivity and what she does to retain serenity.

The following session she was asked if she wanted the intervention to be told to her in five words or five hundred. She said five. She was told, "Rest 100 times per day."

The focus of therapy shifted to how she rests. She was asked for recollections of when she maintained emotional tranquility through surrender, emotional calmness through detachment, serenity through letting go, peace of mind by "turning things over," internal quiet by putting things aside, calmness by doing first things first, satisfaction by agreeing to coexist with discomfort. She was asked about the physical sensations that correlate with rest. At the end of this sequence, she was told she didn't seem to know much about how to rest. She was shown how to do a breathing exercise termed "calming breaths" (Wilson, 1986), and a tape was made for her to listen to daily while she studied carefully and in great detail how her body and mind went about resting. She was told she needed to learn how to telescope resting so that she could rest as fast as she could think.

The following week she reported that when the panic attacks started she said to herself, "I really don't want this to happen, or for it to happen here, but if it's going to happen I'll take the time out for it," and that quickly the panic would dissipate.

This case illustrates how the Ericksonian approach to diagnosis implies a solution and how the act of giving the diagnosis can be elaborated to encompass the main thrust of therapy.

For many phobics, the solution to their problem includes not only staying comfortable when threatened, but also daring to enter the phobic situation.

Principle 3: Get the Individual to Do Something

Erickson once remarked, "When you have a patient with some senseless phobia, sympathize with it, and somehow or other, get them to violate that phobia" (Zeig, 1980, p. 253). To achieve this goal, Erickson often would chunk or fractionate the problem. Two of Erickson's cases offer examples of this approach. The first involved a man who owned his own construction firm but went bankrupt because he was afraid to go into downtown Detroit for fear the tall buildings would fall down and crush him. As Erickson related:

> He was reduced to absolute poverty. He simply could not get along in the city because he believed he had to avoid any building over four stories high for fear it might topple over and crush him. So I asked him in the hypnotic trance state to tell me how high a five-storied building, a six-storied, eight-storied, ten-storied building would be, and how far across the street, how far across the block, each building would reach if it tipped over. I explained to him that if a building were, say, 100 feet high, then it would be perfectly safe for him to walk past it from a distance of 130 feet—the extra 30 feet being added to allow for flying debris. Now he could agree to this logic. It made sense to him.
>
> Next I suggested that he map out the various streets and the various buildings in Detroit and calculate what particular distance away from each building he would have to walk in order to feel safe. What he didn't realize is that I was educating him to walk past each of those buildings. He thought I was educating him in the matter of passing them safely and I was; but in walking past them safely he was first of

all walking past them. Previously he had not been able to go down-town in Detroit for fear the buildings would fall on him. But once we had mapped out the city of Detroit so that he could actually walk here and there, he took great pleasure in walking here and there.

Next we started shading the distances. Instead of requiring 130 to 140 feet of distance for a 100-foot high building, well, he could walk 139 feet from it, 138 feet away from it, 137 feet away from it, 136 feet away from it, 130 feet away from it, and so on, until finally he could walk just 100 feet away from it and do so safely. I also pointed out to him that you can see the building begin to fall and how long will it take a 100-foot-high building to fall all the way to the ground? Just figure it out and during that length of time how far away can you get from that dangerous 100-foot distance? So I introduced another element—the time element—and soon he figured out that he could walk 90 feet away from a 100-foot-high building, because that would still give him enough time to get out of harm's way. But what that man really was doing was gradually getting used to the idea of walking past high buildings from increasingly closer distances (Rossi et al., 1983, pp. 196–198).

It is worth noting that after treating this man's phobia, Erickson referred him for more extensive therapy.

The second case involved a man who was afraid to drive outside Phoenix on the freeway. As Erickson related:

Now what I did with Bob was this, "What happens when you try to drive on the street?" He said, "I faint at the wheel." I asked him if he was sure. He said, "Yes. My heart starts pounding, and I faint." I said, "How do you know?" He said, "I know. I've had friends with me in the car and I've tried and I pass out at the wheel and they've had to take charge."

So my approach to him was, "I'd like to have you go up Black Canyon Highway and note the telephone poles. Drive up to the last telephone pole that you dare drive up to and stop at the side of it. Then look at the next telephone pole. Drive up there about three in the morning. After you've looked at the next telephone pole, start your car up in the forward gear and get it going just fast enough so that when you reach the telephone pole safely, you switch off the ignition and you faint as you go past the telephone pole. When you recover, because your car will slow up and you're on the shoulder there." I knew the highway. "When you recover from the faint, wonder if you can go to the next telephone pole. So put your car into first gear, start it up, release the clutch, and as soon as the engine is really turning, turn off the switch, and see if you get to that third telephone pole before you faint." You know Bob had just a lot of fun, he got some 20 miles. (Haley, 1985, p. 119)

In these cases Erickson illustrated the use of one of the most recent and significant advances in the treatment of phobias, in vivo desensitization. In the practice of in vivo desensitization, phobic individuals enter the phobic situation so that while in it, they realize they can maintain satisfactory psychophysiologic functioning. There are two main approaches to doing desensitization: gradual exposure and flooding. Erickson's work in the first case cited above used gradual exposure; the second case used flooding.

Principle 4: Utilize Confusion and Illogic to Disrupt Maladaptive Sets

According to the Ericksonian approach, symptoms are viewed as behaviors embedded in rigid repeating sequences. Confusion and illogic are used as a means of interrupting the repetitive symptomatic behavior sequence, allowing for a more adaptive response to emerge in response to suggestion. To individuals with a panic-level phobia, any suggestion that they solicit the feelings of panic seems crazy. Yet illogic can be curative. For example, Erickson succeeded in having a woman's phobia slide off her body into a chair (Zeig, 1980).

The handling of a case concerning a woman who experienced panic while driving also illustrates the curative value of illogic. Her heart raced, her legs felt rubbery, she got dizzy, and she was afraid she would pass out. The problem developed after she was hit from behind by a tractor-trailer during a rainstorm. She was married, had children, and had a job. She was on medication for nine months, but she continued to have panic attacks when driving in unfamiliar parts of town, on super highways, or on deserted roadways. Her problem was getting worse and she was concerned that she would lose more and more of her ability to drive.

She was told that she really needed to be able to drive for the sake of her kids and her husband, as well as for herself. Further, she was told that she would be able to drive anywhere she wanted if she were willing to do some hard work and if she agreed to being only reasonably comfortable in the car. She agreed to both these terms.

She was told that the first step toward recovery was to be confident that she could tolerate any panic attack without passing out. No matter how I tried to reassure her that she wouldn't pass out and die, that was something she could only really know through experience. Therefore, I told her that she was to spend one-half hour per day searching for the worst panic attack she could find. She was to get familiar with how a bad panic attack would smell, and how it sounded, and what it tasted like. Each day she should drive until she found a really bad panic attack, then pull off to the side of the road and bring it on fully by inviting it, or challenging it, or daring it to hit her with all that it had. Within one week of this exercise she was confident she could control the bad ones.

Principle 5: Use Social Systems

It is interesting to note that in describing the original formulation of the double-bind theory of schizophrenia, Haley (1981) provides an understanding for the interpersonal foundation of panic attacks: "Once the individual has learned to expect this pattern [double-binds in family communication], almost any part of the double-bind sequence may then be sufficient to precipitate panic or rage" (p. 13). Double-bind induced behavior often continues to be a part of their responses to others.

Phobic individuals characteristically turn to others for reassurance, yet as the double-bind theory would predict, they often reject the leadership offered by the person to whom they turn. The dilemma of the support person is illustrative. The support person is someone who is intimately involved in helping the phobic overcome his or her problem. Often the support person tries a wide variety of strategies to help the phobic. Inevitably, some of these ideas are meritorious but rejected by the phobic. The phobic may not follow through with a plan, or may point out that the support person is not phobic and therefore cannot decide the correct plan of action, and so forth. The support person often gets into the dilemma of being one-up in the relationship by virtue of being nonsymptomatic, while simultaneously being one-down because his or her advice is unsuccessful in helping. Nonetheless, the phobic may continue to expect the support person to be a helper. Often the support person may need to participate in therapy to help the phobic avoid avoiding.

For example, Howard was an ex-Marine whose wife was agoraphobic. In response to the frustration and helplessness he felt in trying to assist his wife, he would get angry at her. Howard was told he couldn't possibly understand what his wife experienced at the moment of panic, nor should he try to. She was told it was her responsibility to educate him about her dilemma so that he did not feel so frustrated and confused about her behavior. He was told that there is no way he could adequately reassure his wife about his caring for her or her ability to overcome the phobia. The best he could do would be to be available as her companion whenever she wanted to practice entering phobic situations. It was suggested that each day as he was leaving the house for work he say to her, "I insist you get over this problem" *and nothing more*. Otherwise, his wife was to be completely in charge of her problem.

Six months later, Howard had not yelled at his wife, and together they had enjoyed a number of successes in her going further into phobic situations.

Since I live in Phoenix I have had contact with several people Erickson once treated for phobic disorders. One of them, Anne, relates that during her first sessions with Erickson he asked about her relationship with her mother and father. After Anne described her mother she told Erickson that her mother was soon to visit Phoenix and she was concerned because no matter how clean the house was, her mother would be critical. Erickson gave her an assignment that on the day before her mother arrived she was to take the curtains down from the windows, roll them in the dirt, then hang them again. Anne reports that she only did the assignment figuratively, but that it was helpful.*

Conclusion

The Ericksonian approach to therapy has characteristics that make it uniquely suited for working with phobias. Erickson's therapy is especially attentive to psychophysiology. The approach emphasizes making the individual aware of what actions he or she is capable of performing. This focus is in line with the primary therapeutic approach currently used with phobias, namely, in vivo desensitization and flooding. The care given to the manner of presenting ideas gives the Ericksonian practitioner leverage in motivating phobics to do what they can do, to stop avoiding their phobias. Much attention needs to be given to elaborating how the Ericksonian approach can be applied to other psychological problems of people with phobias. Its major contributions appear to be its attention to current strengths of the client which can be applied to the problem area and innovative methods of encouraging the client to face the phobic situation. In addition, the clinician utilizing these methods of presenting ideas to the client will discover the elegance of fit between a therapy that utilizes the illogical and a problem based on the irrational.

References

Haley, J. (1976). *Problem-solving therapy*. New York: Harper Lulophan Books.
Haley, J. (1981). *Reflecting on therapy and other essays*. Chevy Chase, MD: The Family Therapy Institute of Washington, DC.

---

*Videotapes of some of Erickson's work with Anne are available at the Erickson Foundation Archives in Phoenix, Arizona.

Haley, J. (1985). *Conversations with Milton H. Erickson, M.D. Volume 1, Changing individuals*. New York: Norton.

Herrigel, E. (1971). *Zen in the art of archery*. New York: Vintage Books.

Rossi, E. L., Ryan, M. D., & Sharp, F. A. (Eds.) (1983). *Healing in hypnosis, the seminars, workshops, and lectures of Milton H. Erickson* (Volume 1). New York: Irvington Publications.

Wilson, R. R. (1986). *Don't panic: Taking control of anxiety attacks*. New York: Harper & Row.

Zeig, J. K. (1980). *A teaching seminar with Milton H. Erickson*. New York: Brunner/Mazel.

Zeig, J. K. (1985a). *Experiencing Erickson: An introduction to the man and his work*. New York: Brunner/Mazel.

Zeig, J. K. (1985b, December). *Therapeutic patterns in Ericksonian psychotherapy*. Paper presented at the Evolution of Psychotherapy Conference, Phoenix.

Charles Van Riper Meets Milton H. Erickson: Approaches in the Treatment of the Adult Stutterer

Bernhard Trenkle, Dipl. Psych.

Bernhard Trenkle, Dipl. Psych. (University of Heidelberg), is one of the leading Ericksonian trainers and practitioners in Germany. He is a member of the Board of Directors of The Milton Erickson Society of Germany and editor of its newsletter. He is also a member of the Editorial Boards of Hypnose und Kognition *and the* Ericksonian Monographs. *Previous publications are on speech therapy, Ericksonian therapy and family therapy and include a co-authored chapter on family therapy in* Ericksonian Psychotherapy, Volume II *(J. Zeig, Ed., Brunner/Mazel, 1985).*

The work of Charles Van Riper, a renowned speech therapist, was influenced by Milton Erickson. Trenkle discovered Van Riper's fascinating work and compares it to Erickson's. He provides several cases to illustrate similarities in the work of these two remarkable therapists.

Four years ago I started working in a speech pathology department where I treated patients with speech and voice problems. Because I had received training in family therapy and had been studying Ericksonian approaches to therapy for many years, I expected to be well prepared for the job. But the limits of my therapeutic repertoire were soon apparent, especially while doing therapy with adult stutterers. The family therapy and psychotherapeutic interventions I had trusted did not seem to work as I had come to expect. For the first time in my career, a noticeable number of patients discontinued therapy prematurely.

I thought back to the time when I treated my first enuretic patient. I had looked up Erickson's case studies of enuretic patients to get ideas I could use for my therapy cases. This time, the results were disappointing. The Ericksonian literature did not provide me with any inspiring ideas and the

Address reprint requests to Bernhard Trenkle, Dipl. Psych., Bahnhofstrasse 4, Rottweil, West Germany.

term "stuttering" appeared only twice in the *Collected Papers* (Erickson, 1980).

Then a speech therapist told me about a book by Charles Van Riper (1979), in which Van Riper uses several impressive case studies to illustrate his therapeutic philosophy based on five decades of experience. I was captured by the book, just as I had been by Jay Haley's *Uncommon Therapy* (1973). After reading Van Riper, I felt that the title *Uncommon Therapy* would have been just as appropriate for his book. I would, therefore, like to introduce this man and his work and use several examples to illustrate the integration of his approach with Erickson's.

Van Riper is known as one of the great pioneers of speech therapy. *Speech Correction* was first printed in 1938 and is in its seventh edition (Van Riper & Emerick, 1982). Van Riper was a stutterer himself and has dedicated most of his professional life to the therapy of stutterers. His approach to therapy is based on the assumption that stuttering occurs intermittently. Phases of severe stuttering alternate with phases of relative fluency of speech. Further, there are factors that affect the frequency and intensity of the stuttering in positive as well as negative ways. Based on these factors, Van Riper formulated his "equation of stuttering":

> The numerator contains the factors which increase the stuttering. Among these are: anxiety, frustration, guilt feelings, fear of certain words or situations, and communicative stress. The denominator shows the factors which decrease the stuttering, such as self-confidence or ego strength. The therapeutic goal is to decrease the factors in the numerator and increase those in the denominator.

He uses the acronym MIDVAS to refer to the six stages of treatment: motivation, identification, desensibilisation, variation, approximation, and stabilization. The first step of this approach is to *motivate* stutterers to undergo therapy. This is necessary because in spite of the disadvantages and the personal suffering involved, avoidance behavior and the fear of being confronted with the symptom are often stronger than the motivation for therapy. During the *identification* phase, a thorough analysis of the symptoms is undertaken. This eventually allows a volitional reproduction of the symptoms, which aids in a reduction of fear and avoidance behavior. During the *desensibilisation* phase, an attempt is made to desensitize the "stutterer soul," at the point of greatest fear and difficulty for each particular stutterer. For one stutterer it may be embarrassment; for another it may be the fear of making phone calls. During the phase of *approximation*, an attempt is made to approximate the goal of being a "fluent stutterer." During the *variation* phase, the therapist helps to establish altered speech patterns and systematically disrupts the old speech patterns. The final phase, of *stabilization*, insures that clients will be able to continue the newly acquired behaviors even in critical situations. Furthermore, they will be able to treat themselves using the same therapeutic techniques, should this ever be required. Much of this is similar to Erickson's approach.

Van Riper is considered a behaviorist. Based on the principles of learning, he practices a symptom-oriented therapy. However, even though many aspects of this approach are, indeed, symptom oriented, a closer look at his work reveals that numerous changes of a different type are also effected. These differences, in many cases, amount to a complete psychotherapy. Due to this apparent similarity to Erickson's therapeutic philosophy and procedures, I wrote Van Riper that I felt he had created an efficient, indirect approach to psychotherapy and asked whether he had been influenced by Dr. Erickson. Van Riper (1983) answered:

> It is interesting that you saw the influence of Erickson in my work. Few people have but I was profoundly fascinated by my reading of his works and I'm sure his insights contributed much to my kind of stuttering therapy. I have been known for my symptomatic treatment of stuttering, but always there has been a basic psychotherapy incorporated within it. In the *Handbook of Speech Pathology* edited by Travis, I have presented this most vividly. I never met Dr. Erickson, though we had several exchanges of letters.

In his chapter in the *Handbook of Speech Pathology*, Van Riper (1973) states: "We tried to develop a therapy which, while masquerading as a symptomatic therapy, would actually be a psychotherapy" (p. 1001).

Like Erickson, Van Riper makes use of a variety of techniques and strategies to accomplish his treatment goals. In this chapter I will compare some specific aspects of their work. For a more detailed discussion of other aspects see Trenkle & Brunner (1986). The areas of comparison include: modeling, personal contact, enhanced perceptions, consideration of ethnic possibilities, utilization of individuals' behavior, and use of stories and symbols.

Modeling

Erickson had to cope with polio and Van Riper had to deal with severe stuttering. As a result of overcoming disabilities both conveyed to others that it is possible to master difficult life situations. Both stressed the importance of positive expectations: "The client cannot have much hope if the clinician has little" (Van Riper, 1979, p. 105). "Deeds are the offspring of hope and expectancy" (Erickson, 1954, p. 262). By conducting their own lives in a therapeutic manner they both embodied hope and exemplified the approach they taught.

Personal Contact

Erickson's therapeutic engagement did not end after the clients left his consulting room. He visited restaurants with his clients or occasionally introduced them to members of his family. For example, for years a young psychotic watched television with him every day for two hours. He interspersed therapeutic communication within the course of casual conversation in his effort to stabilize the young man (Zeig, 1985). In the course of his life Van Riper accepted 14 children in his family. He visited the relatives of clients. In an emergency situation, he even contacted university professors to obtain results of an admission examination for a client (Van Riper, 1979, p. 51). For Erickson and Van Riper, special situations call for special therapeutic actions, and they did not confine themselves to their office.

Enhanced Perceptual Capabilities

Erickson's abilities to observe and then to arrive at the correct diagnostic assessment is legendary. It is said that he could often tell when a secretary was menstruating by the way she typed a letter. Like Erickson, Van Riper worked on developing his perceptual abilities. Van Riper states that some of his students and patients swore that he could read their minds. He claims, though, that these are not god-given abilities, but are "the result of very careful observation, uninhibited inference making, and the calculation of probabilities. It comes through empathy." Van Riper describes how he practiced the art of shadowing speech: "I learned the skill of shadowing the speech of others, saying what they said at almost the same time they said it. First, I did this aloud when listening to speakers on the radio, then covertly when listening to others. I tried to match not only the words, but the tempo, voice inflections and pauses as well. One can also learn to 'shadow' the gestures, postures, and movements of other people almost as actors do in learning a role" (Van Riper, 1979, p. 108). He describes how this practice enabled him to finish incomplete sentences of others and predict what they would say next.

Van Riper talks about a visit to a fortune-teller. He recognized that she first confronted him with a series of statements that were, objectively, either true or false, such as, "It is cold today." This helped her analyze how he expressed agreement or disagreement nonverbally. Once she had recognized these patterns, she talked a lot and "discovered the truth" guided by his minimal nonverbal cues. Van Riper used this strategy successfully while playing poker with his colleagues, until they would agree to play with him only after he had promised to keep his mouth shut (Van Riper, 1979, p. 109).

Similarly, Erickson, relying on his highly developed perceptual and communicative abilities, managed to mislead fortune-tellers and, on one occasion, a researcher of PSI phenomenon (Rosen, 1982).

A short summary of one of Van Riper's case studies may help clarify some of the means by which he used his highly developed perceptual acuity. Teddy was nine years old. He was intelligent, read above his grade level, and did well in school. However, his spontaneous speech was almost unintelligible. Even his parents had trouble understanding him. Especially strange was that in syllables and short words he made every sound perfectly when repeating them, but he could not prolong them at all in isolation. He made strange errors every time he used connected speech. The moment he spoke polysyllabic words or several words together he became almost completely unintelligible.

Teddy was the son of the superintendent of the school where his speech therapist was working. This therapist asked Van Riper for help since her predecessor had been fired when she couldn't help Teddy. This therapist felt that she was not making progress with him either. Van Riper listened to a tape recording of Teddy speaking. On the tape Teddy first said each of the words correctly: "the, girl, likes, to, go, to, the, store." But when he read the same words in a complete sentence, the utterance was incomprehensible. Moreover, his articulation errors were unusual. He substituted "f" for "t" and "d," "k," "g" and "l" for "n" and even had trouble with "b" and "m" sounds, using a distorted "v" as replacement.

Van Riper remarked that he probably knew what the cause was as well as what to do. Teddy's therapist was skeptical and sarcastic and said, "OK, Sherlock Holmes. I'm your Ms. Watson. What do you deduce, Sir?" Van Riper replied, "All right, Ms. Watson. If you will interview Teddy's parents you will find that Teddy is so afraid of water he will not learn to swim, and that he always sleeps with his arms outside the covers and snores loudly. Moreover, he will drink milk at home but not in school. And when he is given an all day sucker, the kind with a stick, he only licks it and will never suck it. He also has had frequent earaches." The therapist remained skeptical and called Mr. Holmes a "monstrous fraud." Van Riper wrote down a few more predictions and sealed these in an envelope.

The therapist was quite amazed when she returned from her interview. Van Riper had predicted everything correctly except the snoring. Even the fact that he'd drink milk at home but wouldn't touch it at school was correct. The other predictions within the sealed envelope, regarding asthma, nasal polyps, deviated septum, and several other medical conditions had also mostly been correct.

Then Van Riper explained what he had observed to the therapist: The boy avoids occluding his oral pathway at all costs. He is afraid that if he does he will not be able to breathe. He is trying to talk without ever blocking his oral pathway. Van Riper discussed Teddy's unusual sound substitutions in great detail, his conspicuous breathing pattern while speaking, and the medical problems that possibly cause these specific symptoms. Then he recounted that one of his patients, a little girl, had shown similar symptoms. She had been treated with a respirator due to polio. This girl told him once, "If I close my mouth, I will die." He had also learned certain details from her, for instance that drinking milk at home from a cup was OK, but never at school with a straw. When this girl was convinced that she could always inhale through her nose even though her mouth was closed, her misarticulations disappeared almost magically.

Van Riper suggested a treatment plan that included techniques based on classical conditioning. Concurrently, Teddy was supposed to receive many positive suggestions through reading, speaking and thinking, such as "I can always breathe through my nose." Van Riper later received a tape recording which demonstrated that Teddy was speaking almost flawlessly.

Consideration of Ethnic Possibilities

Studies of different cultures reveal unique opportunities to analyze complex patterns. Erickson once said, "I think anthropology should be something all psychotherapists should read and know about because different ethnic groups have different ways of thinking about things" (Zeig, 1980, p. 119). Such knowledge can aid in furthering therapists' capabilities.

There are several case studies which show how Erickson utilized his knowledge of different cultures for therapeutic purposes. For instance, a Prussian man had been totally paralyzed for a year due to a stroke and as a result could not talk. Erickson sat down in front of the helpless man and began to talk with him in the following way:

> So you are a Prussian German. The stupid , Goddamn Nazis! How incredibly stupid, conceited, ignorant, and animal-like Prussian Germans are. They thought they owned the world, they destroyed their own country!... You're so Goddamn lazy you're content to lie in a charity bed.

Erickson asked his family to bring the patient back to see him again the next day so that he could really let him know his opinion on these issues. The man finally uttered his first word "No," and left the room, swaying, but without assistance. Erickson utilized the pride of the Prussians and their great sensitivity in order to accomplish this first breakthrough. Several weeks of rehabilitational therapy followed (Haley, 1973, p. 310).

Similarly, several cases show Van Riper's appreciation for ethnic details. A young Chinese came to him for treatment from Hong Kong. Van Riper talked about the difficulties he encountered trying to adapt to the client's different body language and nonverbal patterns. One of the biggest problems was that his patient absolutely refused to analyze and investigate his own pattern of stuttering. When placed in front of a mirror to observe his stuttering, he dashed out of the office and did not return for two weeks. Three weeks later a frustrated Van Riper went to an Oriental restaurant owned by a friend, who explained that one of the basic Chinese values was "to live so as to be a credit to oneself, to one's family and to one's ancestors. Stuttering was a disgraceful act, completely unacceptable." The owner continued, "There are two kinds of face (pride), *lien* and *mien*, one referring to the self and the family, and the other to the ancestors. When Chang stutters, a thousand ancestors turn over in their graves and lie face down." Van Riper observed, "All severe stutterers find it hard to confront their stuttering behaviors objectively, but at least they don't have a thousand ancestors turning face down in their graves when they do so" (1979, p. 104).

This information finally led to the breakthrough in therapy. Van Riper had the patient watch a videorecording of his stuttering while in a state of relaxation: 1) with eyes half closed and with the sound off; 2) with eyes closed but the sound turned on; 3) with eyes open and the sound on; 4) counting all stutterings; and 5) categorizing them into different classes, and so on. It is interesting to note that the first three steps of the above hierarchy are characterized by a dissociation of the sensory channels and resemble Erickson's technique when helping patients approach traumatic events in trance.

The treatment of Abdul, a stuttering Arab, is equally fascinating. Van Riper studied books on the Arabic culture and the Koran. According to the Koran, God will only be in a man, if he leads life consciously and in full control of self. If not Al Kohol, the devil, dwells in him. This explains why epileptics and those suffering from cerebral palsy are rejected in the Arabic culture. While he was growing up Abdul was excluded by others for the same reasons. Van Riper eventually managed to convince Abdul to study the Koran and the Islamic tradition seriously and to seek his own religious path. Afterwards Abdul began explaining his belief to Van Riper and would try to convince him to convert to Islam. Whenever he did this most of his stuttering would disappear. When Van Riper pointed this out to the patient, Abdul said, "Of course, it is Allah speaking, not me! Allah does not stutter."

Van Riper's procedure at this point is most interesting. His goal was "to keep Allah inside Abdul's mouth and to keep Al Kohol out." For the next three days, Van Riper and his patient carried out every gesture and movement consciously. This began while eating: Everytime Abdul lifted the spoon to his mouth, it was done consciously. He even scratched his head consciously. All gestures and movements that usually took place automatically were now conscious. Every word spoken and every step taken were turned into a volitional act. Van Riper describes the great effort required as well as the tremendous feeling of power which ensued. Never before and never after had he experienced such a feeling of omnipotence and inner strength. Abdul was experiencing similar feelings and said without stuttering, "Allah is in me! I feel him. I am not afraid. I can speak." This was the turning point in therapy.

Abdul underwent a most remarkable metamorphosis. He really worked on his stuttering, hard and successfully. "From the furtive, suspicious, stuttering cocoon there emerged a tremendous man—strong, confident, outgoing—who has since done great deeds. I have been amazed to view his achievements" (Van Riper, 1979, p. 116).

Utilization of Individuals

Both Erickson and Van Riper stressed that every patient is a unique individual. "I think that true psychotherapy is knowing that each patient is an individual, unique and different" (Erickson in Zeig, 1980, p. 226). "If we tailor the therapy to the stutterer's unique needs—and they are always unique— we must be able to appraise the kind of a person and the kind of a problem he presents" (Van Riper, 1973, p. 219).

An underlying principle of Erickson's work is the principle of utilization. Utilization is based on the recognition that individual patterns of behavior and thought can be relied upon to achieve therapeutic goals. This includes the utilization of seemingly problematic aspects of a client's personality. A well-known example demonstrating this principle is Erickson's case of a young man who stated he was Jesus and who tried to convert other patients on the psychiatric ward. Erickson said, "I understand you have had experience as a carpenter?" Since the client operated from this frame of reference he had no choice but to agree. Erickson soon asked him to build a bookshelf in the ward and eventually led him to other useful and productive activities (Haley, 1973, p. 28).

Utilization is also an underlying principle of Van Riper's work as can be seen in his treatment of Abdul, and in his work with Tex. Tex, a professional gambler, was a severe stutterer with long silent laryngeal blockings. In the beginning of treatment he could not formulate speech. Van Riper spent hours with this client in silent frustration. In desperation, Van Riper and the patient went to a bar and, after drinking, a different personality emerged. Tex told Van Riper that at one time he had been a locomotive fireman. His stuttering had caused a train wreck in which several people, including children, were killed. He had been unable to warn the engineer of the danger he had seen coming. Each time he thought of the wreck and the dead children he experienced laryngeal blocking. This basic insight was pivotal, yet not sufficient to free the patient from his stuttering. It was difficult for Tex to produce these laryngeal blocks voluntarily. Although the patient trusted Van Riper, he could not accomplish what Van Riper asked him to do.

Van Riper took this professional gambler to an evening meeting where he played poker with faculty members. They were all enthusiastic about the game but amateurs. Van Riper describes how he motivated the gambler to develop a new speech behavior: "I told Tex we'd invented a new house rule just for him. Every time he put a chip in the pot, he had to say something, and every time he stuttered in his old hard way, we could take a chip from his stack. Well, Tex just could not bear having neophytes and suckers take his gambling money from him—which we did without mercy or loving kindness—so finally he did begin to modify his stuttering and skinned us thoroughly by the end of the evening! He progressed rapidly from then on."

This represents an interesting illustration of the principle of utilization. The patient's strengths, personal motives, honor as a professional gambler, and passion for the game are utilized to finally overcome his traumatic memories and fears. Anxieties and feelings of guilt are kept out of therapeutic focus. Tex's behaviors and attitudes were effectively utilized to overcome a stagnate state. This case of Van Riper also illustrates Erickson's opinion that every patient has the resources necessary for solving his or her problems if properly engaged by the therapist.

Use of Stories

Van Riper repeatedly emphasized that therapists working with stutterers will meet strong resistance and that motivating these patients for therapy is of great importance. When working on reducing strong resistance or severe avoidance, or merely moving toward therapeutic goals, I often use Ericksonian techniques, especially stories and symbols. Van

Riper also uses marvelous stories both in teaching and in training. In order to treat silent patients, for instance, he recommends talking about patients who had similar problems and describing how they received help, until the actual patient slowly starts communicating (Van Riper, 1979, p. 9). Ericksonian therapists are generally familiar with this strategy, as many books have been published focusing on his use of stories and metaphors (Gordon, 1978; Lankton & Lankton, 1983; Mills & Crowley, 1986; Rosen, 1982; Watzlawick, 1978; Zeig, 1980). The following examples illustrate how I use stories when working with stutterers.

Daring to Look at One's Face

As several case studies have shown, it is extremely difficult for many stutterers to be confronted with their own stuttering by a mirror or through a videorecording. Reactions such as sweating, crying and covering one's face with one's hands are not at all uncommon. Such behavior was reduced considerably after I started telling my (usually hypnotized) patients the following story adapted from Shah (1978).

And there is this lion living in the rugged woods where strong winds blow all the time. He has a pool full with cool, fresh water. However, a strong wind is always blowing. There are always ripples on the surface of the water. And the water never reflects any light. Always ripples. One day the lion goes out to hunt. And it is such a delightful feeling to hunt. Hour after hour. There is a wonderful experience of rhythm, he finds a regular, calm rhythm in his movements and his breathing. And he is so absorbed, hunting, that he forgets everything around him. More and more. There is just the rhythm. His goal. So totally absorbed, that he doesn't notice, that he is moving out of the woods, farther and farther. And finally, his needs, so far away from his water, cool and delicious. But lions can smell. They smell water across vast distances. And he catches the scent of water: wonderful fresh water. And he is running toward it. And there is a small lake. Fresh water. Not a breeze. Smooth, like a mirror. And he runs toward it, he wants to drink. When his head is above the water, he sees the other lion there. And he withdraws and feels annoyed. Why would this water belong to another lion? After some time he goes back thinking that the other lion has left some time ago. But as soon as his head is above the water, there is this other lion again. After a brief retreat he decides to chase the other one away. He starts running toward the lake, opens his mouth wide, and roars as loudly as he can. But the other lion opens his mouth wide as well and his roar is equally terrible. When he approaches the lake for the fourth time a rather frightened lion looks back at him. And there he is—with all of his needs—lying down. But, somewhere along the line, he rises, thinks, "So what? Who cares about that lion?" He puts his head into the water; ripples appear on the water, and no longer is there another lion.

In story telling, interventions are tailored so they fit the needs of the individual patient. Aside from the basic theme of the story, which above is to overcome fear by simply putting one's head into the water, to risk a new experience, it can be modified according to the client's specific needs. If a client is embarrassed by symptoms, the lion can be embarrassed as well about his lack of courage. If a client is exhausted due to a long, hard day of work, the lion can rest after drinking from the water and begin his way back in a refreshed, relaxed state. On his way back, he starts perceiving the scenery in a new, different way. After his experience at the water hole he feels confident, self-assured, invigorated with a new type of strength. For a client who revels in feelings of anger and frustration, the lion could feel annoyed that he let things get this far. His need for water gets stronger and stronger until the lion finally decides to rise and act in a new and different way. And so on.

Cooperation with Others

In a three day group therapy setting for adult stutterers, a speech therapist and I offered exercises aimed at building up new patterns of speech. Several group members were having difficulties with the exercises when one man expressed his unwillingness to deal with the problems of the others: "I don't understand why we don't do individual therapy right away since everyone's problems are different anyway. I feel that by listening to the stuttering of others I get even worse and my own stuttering increases. Each of us is different and everyone needs 'special foods.'" The metaphor of "special food" reminded me of a story by Peseschkian (1979) and I asked the speech therapist to make a few copies of it. When she returned the discussion about group vs. individual therapy had ended. We used the following story as a reading exercise and each group member got to read it twice. The following is a shortened version of the story.

A man asked the prophet Elias about the difference between paradise and hell. The prophet takes him to a large room. In the center of the room, there is a big cast iron pot above the fire. There is a hot soup that smells delicious in that steaming hot pot. But one can hear a constant screaming and crying. Many people are trying to eat soup with their spoons, which are six feet long. The spoons are made of cast iron and have wooden handles. But they are too long and too heavy. Therefore, the people burn themselves while trying to hold their spoon. Some hit each other with their spoons. All of them are screaming from pain and hunger. The prophet says, "You see, this is hell!" Then they go to the next room, which is just like the first. The same pot, the same delicious smells, even the same spoons. But everything is quiet and peaceful. There are always two people holding the spoon while a third is carefully sipping soup. Elias the prophet says, "You see this is paradise."

When I entered the group room the next morning I heard two members who had previously avoided each other, talking to one another: "What did you say? Which letters do you have trouble with?" One of these patients was in a managerial position and demanded too much of himself. After reading the story he began delegating duties to co-workers. For the patients this story had served as more than practice material for their speech and voice exercises. It is an example of how contents of metaphoric stories become effective on an unconscious level.

Accepting Varying Phases

Stuttering is not consistent. Phases of relative fluency alternate with phases of increased stuttering. Early progress in therapy may be disrupted by phases of increased stuttering so that the initial euphoria turns into skepticism. There is also a tendency among stutterers to overemphasize "good phases" and to suffer a total loss of self-confidence during "bad phases." In order to induce a more realistic overall appraisal of progress during these phases, I use a story of Till Eulenspiegel (a popular character of German folklore), which has been slightly modified to fit therapeutic purposes.

Till is hiking in the lower foothills. He is walking uphill. It is cold and raining. His path is narrow and full of thorns. Till is humming a tune in a cheerful mood. He knows that this can't go on indefinitely. Sooner or later, the sun will be shining and the path will be straight and easy to walk on. And soon enough the sun comes out and it gets warm. The path slopes gently downhill. And Till starts sobbing and crying. He knows that this cannot continue indefinitely. Sooner or later, there will be thorns again, the path will go steeply uphill, it will be cold, it will rain. And, indeed, after awhile the path is steep again.

And he is humming and singing, because he knows that the cold and the thorns will not be there forever...

It is interesting to observe that clients traditionally adopt the attitude portrayed in this story. However, a spontaneous amnesia for the story itself occurs more often than with other stories I have used. The process of "forgetting" is indirectly addressed since the story teaches not forgetting the bad times during the good times and vice versa. I do not understand why clients tend to forget this story while implementing the lesson it conveys. Nevertheless, it produces a therapeutic transition through an important phase of treatment.

Symbolic Therapy

Another aspect of Ericksonian therapy is the use of symbols (see, for example, "Symbolic Hypnotherapy," a videotape from the Milton H. Erickson Foundation). Van Riper also uses symbols. Here is an assignment he gave to a stuttering patient: "You've reported how frequently you keep reviewing your wrongs and hates. This evening before you go to bed write out as many of them as you can on toilet tissue, read them again, then flush them down the drain" (Van Riper, 1968). Van Riper uses this task during the variation phase while working on issues like fear, guilt, and aggression. The way in which he goes about this task is symbolic. Toilet tissue is there for only one purpose; afterwards you flush it down and leave it behind.

Occasionally I also use symbols in my work with stutterers: A 28-year-old ambitious lawyer complained about his speech difficulties in specific situations. Usually he talked rather freely. However, in social situations when he felt under pressure, he started speaking rapidly and began to stutter. He felt he had sufficient control in various work situations and during sports activities. But not when his father-in-law engaged him in heavy discussions.

I used the analogy that his father-in-law was evidently capable of pulling the plug of his self-esteem. Like when one pulls out the plug of a sink, his self-esteem would go down the drain. His self-esteem would disappear instantly. I told him two examples of successful therapies using symbols and gave him an assignment. He was to purchase a bathtub plug with a chain. He was to carry it with him in his pocket and to approach his father-in-law directly. He was to touch the plug and pay attention to exactly when and how his father-in-law managed to pull the plug out. He was to continue to carry the plug everywhere so he would always remember that he was someone whose plug could be pulled and whose whole self-esteem would then go into the gutter.

He returned three weeks later, showed me the plug, and explained that his father-in-law had not managed to make him stutter, not even when they once met unexpectedly and he did not have the plug with him.

This assignment included other elements besides the use of symbol. The task to approach his father-in-law directly included a paradoxical prescription of the symptom, and the remark that he was someone whose self-esteem "plug" could be pulled at any time was a provocative statement for a man with his ambition. Thus, his values were utilized, according to the principle of utilization of individuals, in order to accomplish his therapeutic goals.

Conclusion

The similarities between the work of Milton H. Erickson and the renowned speech therapist, Charles Van Riper, whose work was influenced by Erickson, are extraordinary. The most obvious is that Van Riper, like Erickson, conducts a complete psychotherapy which masquerades as a symptom-oriented approach. Parallels exist in several distinct areas: modeling therapeutic success; relying upon enhanced perceptual capabilities; the consideration of ethnic possibilities; utilization of individual idiosyncrasies to formulate intervention; using stories to reduce resistance, and symbolic interventions. Case examples from the works of Erickson and Van Riper are cited as well as from my own practice.

References

Erickson, M. H. (1954). Pseudo-orientation in time as a hypnotherapeutic procedure. *Journal of Clinical and Experimental Hypnosis, 2*, 261–283.

Erickson, M. H. (1980). *The collected papers of Milton H. Erickson* (Vols. I–IV, E. L. Rossi, Ed.). New York: Irvington.

Gordon, D. (1978). *Therapeutic Metaphors.* Cupertino, CA: Meta.

Haley, J. (1973). *Uncommon therapy: The psychiatric techniques of M. H. Erickson, M.D.* New York: Norton.

Lankton, S., & Lankton, C. (1983). *The answer within.* New York: Brunner/Mazel.

Mills, J. C., Crowley, R. (in collaboration with Ryan, M. O.). (1986). *Therapeutic metaphors for children and the child within.* New York: Brunner/Mazel.

Peseschkian, N. (1979). *Der Kaufmann und der Papagei: Orientalische Geschichten als Medien in der Psychotherapie.* Frankfurt: Fischer.

Rosen, S. (1982). *My voice will go with you.* New York: Norton.

Shah, I. (1978). *A perfumed scorpion.* London: Octagon Press.

Trenkle, B., & Brunner, M. (1986). Moeglichkeiten in der Behandlung der Sprechangst nach Charles Van Riper und Milton H. Erickson: Prinzipien und Techniken. In G. Lotzmann (Ed.), *Sprechangst in ihrer Beziehung zu Kommunikationsstoerungen.* Berlin: Marhold.

Van Riper, C. (1968). *Speech correction* (6th ed.). Englewood Cliffs, NJ: Prentice-Hall.

Van Riper, C. (1973a). *The treatment of stuttering.* Englewood Cliffs, NJ: Prentice-Hall.

Van Riper, C. (1973b). Symptomatic treatment of stuttering. In L. Travis (Ed.), *Handbook of speech pathology* (pp. 995–1007). Englewood Cliffs, NJ: Prentice-Hall.

Van Riper, C. (1979). *A career in speech pathology.* Englewood Cliffs, NJ: Prentice-Hall.

Van Riper, C. (1983, November 11). Personal communication.

Van Riper, C. & Emerick, L. (1982). *Speech correction: An introduction to speech pathology and audiology* (7th ed.). Englewood Cliffs, NJ: Prentice-Hall.

Watzlawick, P. (1978). *The language of change.* New York: Basic Books.

Zeig, J. (Ed.). (1980). *A teaching seminar with Milton H. Erickson.* New York: Brunner/Mazel.

Zeig, J. (1985). *Experiencing Erickson: An introduction to the man and his work.* New York: Brunner/Mazel.

A "Lavender Duster" Considers The "Purple Sage": Ericksonian Approaches with Homosexuals and Lesbians

Susan H. Mullarky, M.A.

Susan Mullarky, M.A. (Antioch University, Seattle) conducts a private practice and provides consultation training specializing in family therapy, hypnotherapy and issues of homosexuality. She resides in Bothell, Washington.

Mullarky presents a gay therapist's view of therapy. She gives a sensitive account of the treatment of three cases skillfully and successfully handled in the Ericksonian tradition.

I was puzzled as to why I was totally entranced with Ericksonian therapy when, according to my perceptions, Ericksonian "requirements" seemed entirely beyond my grasp. I felt outweighed by the intellectual capacities of Erickson's followers. I had a profound inability to observe intently and knowingly the minute details so importantly elaborated. The complexities and subtleties of language failed to reveal themselves to me. I was "gay" and Milton was "a family man." Important learnings didn't come to me in a "blinding flash of light"; rather they accumulated like dust — slowly, inexorably, pervasively.

Finally I figured out why I persisted with such dogged determination to understand Ericksonian therapy. I believed what he taught. I believed in "his willingness to let people teach him what was real or true about themselves" (Havens, 1985, p. 7). I believe "what is needed is the development of a therapeutic situation permitting the patient to use his own thinking, his own understanding, his own emotions in the way that best fit him in his scheme of life" (Erickson, 1980, p. 223). So this "lavender

Address reprint requests to Susan H. Mullarky, 17502 113th NE, Bothell, WA 98011.

duster," having reconciled within herself all the seemingly insurmountable obstacles, would like to share some thoughts about Ericksonian therapy and the Gay Community.

In the Closet

Myths or misunderstandings about gays and the Gay Community abound. Some of the myths are theories attempting to prove there is a "cause" for homosexuality, thereby setting the stage for a "cure." Some of the myths can be vehicles for expressing prejudice and hate, masking internal and external fears.

Many of the misconceptions are so much a part of the fabric of our American culture that they are outside of our conscious awareness. It is said that gay men and women come from broken families, or experienced sexual trauma at an early age. Or that gay men and women are afraid of sexual relations with the opposite sex. Or that homosexuality results from some physical or genetic deformity, is a mental illness, is an arrested stage of development. Or that it is possible to change your sexual orientation. It is said that gay men and women prefer sex with children. Or that gay women hate men and gay men hate women, or that gay women want to be men or gay men want to be women. Some people believe these ideas are true. While they may be true for some gay people, they are not true of being gay. From my clinical and personal experience these seem to be figments of our cultural imagination.

Gay people are considered "in the closet" when they hide all or part of their sexual identity from others. Some of the most important steps taken by gay men and women are called "coming out." To "come out" is to identify first to yourself that you are gay, and then to others: your family-of-origin, your friends, perhaps co-workers, your lover, and if you or your lover have children, the children. Coming out is risky and important. Therapists need to be ready to support gay clients' coming out, but it is always up to the clients to decide whom to tell and when.

Only the clients can safely gauge the risks. They know best the prejudices and biases of their culture in regard to homosexuality. They are the ones who have to bear the losses, not the therapist. There is a very high likelihood that in coming out, friends and/or family members will be lost.

Often "straight" therapists do not appreciate the danger coming out entails. Yet therapists only need to listen to the TV, to the radio, to read the paper about the climate today in regard to the Gay Community to appreciate the danger that gays feel. The Supreme Court recently upheld sodomy laws. A man who believes gay people ought not to exist is running for president. Worse, there is AIDS, and a belief that homosexuals represent not only a threat to morality, but also a threat to life itself.

Some gay women and men literally live two lives. Depending on the context they dress differently, act differently, and speak a different language. It is not as though these people split their lives in a dissociative manner, it is more like a shifting of gears. A chameleon changes its colors in order to enhance its chances to survive in a particular environment. In many contexts gay people must resemble chameleons to survive in environments that are perceived as hostile. And much of the world is hostile to gays.

Still, many gays believe that coming out has therapeutic benefits despite the risks. Anyone who is "in the closet" has to act as if they are straight. Gays who are in the closet at work feel torn every time they confront that innocuous Monday morning question, "What did you do this weekend?" If they wish to share experiences without coming out they need to speak very carefully, changing gender pronouns and using gender neutral language. If they wish not to misrepresent themselves they need to avoid social conversation with co-workers.

Gays who have not come out to their families go home for family holidays without their mates. They lie or avoid conversation about dates and marriage plans. They attend their parents' funerals without their partner's support. They have to avoid opportunities to reveal themselves more intimately to family members.

Gay couples who have chosen to parent children feel acutely the dilemma of coming out versus staying in the closet. If they are not "out," the coparent has no socially recognized role with the children, cannot deal with school problems, authorize emergency medical care, etc. Children of gay parents who are in the closet may be confused by teasing when other children recognize their family as gay, but they cannot turn to their parents for clarification or support. On the other hand, gay parents who come out are vulnerable to losing their children.

Gay partners who are in the closet find themselves suddenly invisible if their partner dies. Family members assume responsibility for their "unmarried" son or daughter, and the obituary, funeral arrangements, and settlement of the estate all reflect the family's relationship to the deceased, without reference to the gay partner.

Unmarried straight couples share some of these problems. However, unlike homosexual couples, heterosexual couples have the option to protect their relationship via marriage; in fact, in some states common laws automatically treat heterosexual partnerships as marriages after a certain number of years. The latent and manifest homophobia of many families prevents them from according their grown child's gay relationship the respectful priority given to married couples. Thus, even very stable, long-term gay relationships can find themselves subject to sudden disconfirmation.

Coming Out

When a gay man or woman is "out" then all the positive aspects of being gay can be emphasized. They can associate with gay friends. They can have love and support from their parents and siblings. They can protect themselves with wills. They can have legal documents that allow them to act on their lover's behalf in times of emergency. They can see their lover in the hospital and be granted "family access." They can be empowered to make life and death decisions for their lover or their children.

The following case studies tell the stories of some gay people who have been my clients. These cases deal not only with "gay" issues but also with a variety of "life" problems. They are also stories about Ericksonian therapy, which provides a framework for matching the therapeutic climate to each client's personal world, and intervening directly and indirectly to access idiosyncratic resources for growth and change.

Graduation Day

A 52-year-old gay man was referred to me for hypnotherapy. He had developed a distressing symptom that appeared during the process of revealing his homosexuality. The problem began when he started dating men. He was unable to sustain an erection whenever he attempted to have a sexual relationship with his date. In fact, he was unable to have an erection at all. To his dismay, at the most important moment in his life, he was impotent.

He went to a gay psychiatrist recommended by the gay hotline. Unfortunately, after several months of therapy he was no better. He was then referred to a sex therapist who was very comfortable working with gay men. He went through an eight-week behavior modification program, but that also failed. He went back to the gay psychiatrist, terrified that he was never going to be able to have the sex life he had dreamed about all his life. The gay psychiatrist decided that hypnotherapy might be helpful and I was contacted. He explained the problem and asked if I would be willing to work with this client. The psychiatrist said that the client was anxious about working with a woman due to the nature of the problem. I said that I would be glad to work with this client and I would be respectful of our gender differences.

Tex was a tall, slim, wide-shouldered, rugged-looking man. He had beautiful silver hair, and a full black mustache. He was dressed in Western clothes from hat to cowboy boots. I remarked about his cowboy hat saying that I had been a rancher once and really liked wearing cowboy hats. He was surprised and delighted to hear that. He talked about what life was like for a cowboy and I talked about life as a cowgirl. We compared what ranching had been like for a city girl versus a country boy. He had all the "natural learning" because he was raised on a farm. I had to work at learning ranching because I was raised in town. He always knew just what to do without conscious effort because he had been taught since childhood all about ranching. He talked about the one-room schoolhouse he had attended; I talked about the large city schools I attended. We both talked about dating and how awful it had been to always date the wrong person. We had both learned to make the right moves and get the right results even though it was with the wrong person.

As we talked I began to realize that perhaps the problem was that Tex simply hadn't got the "rite learnin." He had been to school on the straight dating game but he had not been to school and learned the gay dating game. So I talked about learning and how we learn and wondered how he learned. He learned slowly. He believed in the school of "hard knocks." He needed time to repeat his lessons over and over until he got it just right. He was a "hands on" man and not a "book learnin" fellow.

I decided to continue therapy with an assignment. To give Tex a better idea of what his assignment would be like we discussed how a young gay boy might act or explore sexually in grade school. He might play a prank on his friend. He might wrestle with him; he might offer him part of his lunch. He certainly would hang around with him a great deal. They would share secrets about what boys are all about and talk about what girls are like. They might even show each other their secret parts and pee together on something that caught their fancy. They would do all those things and more. Since Tex had been a boy once, he knew far better than I did all the possibilities of learning that he needed to consider.

His first assignment was to stop everything he was currently attempting to overcome the problem. He was even to stop masturbating. He could think about anything and everything, but he was to physically do nothing. If he had an erection he was to ignore that and act as though nothing was going on. He was to locate all the gay bars in town and then drive by them all. He was not to get out of his car and go in any of them. I told him that I knew it was going to be extremely difficult not to go in any of them; however, he had told me that he learned slowly and needed time to learn correctly. He questioned me about not masturbating. I was most emphatic that he had to ignore what was going on and pay attention to his new learning. This was the school of hard knocks and he was just going to have to take his lumps. He agreed. We set an appointment for the next week.

The following week he reported that he had driven by all the gay bars. He reported that there were several he really would have liked to have gone into, but he had stayed in his car the entire time. He said that he parked his car in front of two different Leather Bars and watched for hours all those handsome hunks going in and out of those bars. He reported that while watching all those handsome men he got excited. He was very tempted to masturbate but restrained himself. He said that he kept reminding himself that he was in school and he had to take his lumps as he learned.

This session lasted about 20 minutes. He was given his next lesson. He was to select two or three gay bars and go into them. He could only talk to the bartender. He could talk to bartenders as long as he wanted, but he was not to start a conversation with anyone else in the bar. Since he was so old, it was doubtful that any of those hunks he saw would want to talk to him. However, if someone mistook him for someone else he could talk to him. No touching! Just talking.

We discussed how this new activity might parallel learning in a particular grade in school. It was decided that it paralleled sixth and seventh grade learning. He was again instructed to imagine all the sexual learning a sixth and seventh grade gay boy might have to experience in order to graduate to the next grade. He was emphatically reminded not to masturbate.

The next week he returned and reported with delight that not only had he talked to bartenders in all three bars, he had also been mistaken for someone else. It seemed there was a great deal of mistaken identity by the young men in these bars. Not only did they talk to him, but they kept touching him. Some even wanted to do more than that. He laughingly said that he had not quite followed all my instructions to the limit. He confessed he had returned the touching a number of times, but he did refuse to go home with any of them. He confessed that he was very tempted. Again we discussed the grade level he might reach next week. Tex thought maybe he might graduate to ninth grade.

Well, in ninth grade some tentative touching might be appropriate so this week he could talk to the bartender, talk to anyone in the bar, and could even have limited contact. Hugging and kissing would be the limit. He could not go home with any of those handsome young men, and he still could not masturbate no matter how difficult or how tempted he was. He had to restrain himself until he graduated. What he needed to do was imagine fully what a ninth or even a tenth grader would do. He could do that all he wanted. Since this was a difficult assignment and there was a great deal to learn, he was to return in two weeks.

Two weeks later he burst into my office joyfully telling me that again he had defied me! He had followed my instructions to the letter until three nights ago when he simply could not contain himself any longer. A particularly handsome young man invited him to go home with him and he agreed. They never made it home. They stopped a few blocks from the bar and engaged in sexual contact to such an extent that Tex was convinced his presenting problem had been resolved.

Erickson understood that the unconscious mind knows how to solve a problem and it is the therapist's task to help set that process in motion: "Your unconscious mind can learn without letting you know it is learning; but at the right time and in the right situation it will shove up into the conscious mind the essential knowledge" (Erickson, 1985, p. 47).

Two Pink Carnations

This next case was rippled with idiosyncratic behavior. It was full of twists and turns, illustrating how myths are internalized by client and therapist alike.

A gay woman came to me for help because she had some problems with her lover. We wandered vaguely for two sessions getting no closer to the problems. Each question I asked with the hope of shedding some light on the problems was skillfully absorbed by Tammy. She would smile seductively, start to answer, then veer off onto a completely different subject that was so interesting I forgot what my question was. At the end of the second session I confessed that I was in need of additional information. Since the problems were between her and her lover I wanted her lover to come with her to the next session. This suggestion was met with a concrete, "No, she won't come in for the next session. She doesn't believe in therapy. She thinks all therapists are nuts. Besides she doesn't think she has any problems."

I would not take no for an answer and said that if she failed to enlist the aid of Chris, I would give Chris a call. I let Tammy know that I seldom failed in enlisting the aid of a lover. Tammy called mid-week to say that Chris had decided to show up at the next session. I thanked her and said that I was looking forward to meeting Chris.

Tammy arrived first. We were in my office passing time by chatting, when I became aware of a roaring noise coming from the front of my office. "Oh," said Tammy, "that will be Chris. She rides a motorcycle." Since this was Chris's first time at the office I excused myself and said that I would go meet her. I was barely to the reception area when the office door flew open so hard it drove the door stop into the wall. Framed in that space was six feet of black human form: black motorcycle helmet, black leather jacket, black pants, and black boots. Black leather hands reached up, jerked off the chin strap, grasped the black helmet, ripped it off and tucked it under a black leather arm. Blue eyes that seemed to be emanating pure hate found me. She stomped forward two steps, leaned toward me and snarled, "Who the #$%%$ are you? I'm supposed to see some #$%&$% shrink! Tammy's here. Her car is here. Where the #$%&$% is she?"

I was intimidated. I tried to speak but nothing worked. I realized that my legs were sending desperate signals that they were failing. I was terrified! "Oh my God, this must be Chris." She stomped a few more steps closer to me. "Oh dear God, she is going to hit me." I carefully raised my left hand and pointed in the general direction of my office. Cotton-mouthed, I squeaked, "Tammy's in there." Chris stomped by me, down the hall, and into my office. At that point I collapsed into a chair. All the wild stories I had heard about violent people zoomed through my mind. "Oh dear God, what was I going to do? I am such a chicken." My heart was pounding violently and I was shaking from the adrenaline jolt that had coursed through my body when my office door crashed open. It was still open, stuck to the wall. So I got up and wobbled over to the door. On the third tug it broke free and I closed the door. I leaned against the door trying to calm down and decide what to do. Thoughts tumbled around in my head: leave, call the police, faint and be carried away, and so on. Then I remembered what a teacher of mine had told me: "With desperate people tell the truth. Lying only escalates the situation." With that thought I made my legs move the rest of me toward my office.

Shaking like a leaf, I entered my office. Chris was sitting in the chair I customarily take so I pulled up a small bench I had and gratefully col-lapsed on it. Catching my breath I put out my right hand in a gesture of supplication and spoke or rather squeaked, "If I say the slightest tiniest word that might possibly offend you, please, please tell me immediately! I promise that I will do my utmost best to use different words. I will stop talking! Oh, my God you look so angry. If I have done the slightest thing to offend you, I apologize. If I do anything in the future that offends you, please tell me instantly and I will stop.

"You see, I am a great big chicken. My middle name is PEEP in capital letters 30 feet high. Bright neon yellow ones blinking PEEP…PEEP. I also have this problem when I really get frightened. My bladder doesn't work right and I have a tendency to faint. So, please, I will be very careful, but I need help. You have to tell me when I am doing something wrong or have gone too far. I do not want you leaping out of your chair and socking me."

As I spoke my plea I watched Chris. The intense hateful glare changed into a look of astonishment. She looked at her lover and then back at me. When I was done she said, "Hell, I'm not angry, I'm scared. I'm afraid that you will think I am a nut. You know, one of those mental cases. I was afraid that you would lock me up."

"You mean that you are not angry? Good Lord, woman, you sure had me fooled! I thought you were going to beat my poor puny body into a different shape! You sure do that scared routine well. I would have sworn on a stack of Bibles 100 feet high that you were angry. You will have to forgive me for a while if I continue to act terrified—my body still wants to run away."

Chris again looked at her lover and then back at me. "Well, it's like this. I'd been to a shrink once before. That #$&%$# creep put me in a nut hospital. They shot me up with all these drugs and then the #$&%$# gave me shock treatments. The #$&%$# treatments took my mind away for a long time. I'd been doing drugs heavy and was acting wild like. So I busted a few people. Then I busted a few in the hospital and that was when they said I was crazy. Tammy made me promise no more drugs and I've been clean since I've been with her. We've been together four years. I'll die and take a few with me before anyone #$&%$# with my mind again!"

"Listen Chris," I said, "I am not a shrink. I am a counselor. I can't put anyone in the nut house. Honest, I have no power to do that."

As I had listened to her brief story I realized that Chris had courage. I doubt if I would have had the courage to show up. No wonder her defenses were in high gear. I also decided to very careful. I was still nervous and more than a bit spooked. My heart was still pounding.

I decided a safe place to begin was to ask Chris if she would mind imagining a scale from 1 to 100. This scale was used to indicate what someone felt like when they came into counseling: 0 was pretty bad and 100 was very good. I asked her if she would mind thinking where she was on this pretend scale and telling me.

Chris quickly answered "6." I misheard her and repeated the number 60. "No," she said, "s-i-x." I started to giggle. I knew it was a reaction to horror, so I smothered the giggle and tried to take in 6. I started to ask what she said again and realized that I might offend her and she would get up and sock me. Again my heart went into overdrive. So I asked her where she might be on this pretend scale when she was done with counseling? She didn't hesitate a blink of an eye and replied "8." Again I misheard her and repeated 80? "No," she said, "e-i-g-h-t." A large silence filled the office. I was speechless. I simply was unable to take in her evaluation.

Tammy broke the silence. She told Chris to tell me what the problem was, since that was why they were here.

With that order from her lover, Chris told me what the problem was. She was Tammy's lover. They shared a bed and bedroom. There were also three other women that lived in their house. She told me they all belonged to the same motorcycle club. They all worked. They all paid their share of the rent. They all got along well. Tammy needed them to help out with several businesses she had on the side. The problem, Chris said, was she could not figure out a way to keep these women from coming in and out of her and Tammy's bedroom. They came in whenever they wanted. Never knocked, just walked in. It was hard to have privacy. After all she was Tammy's lover and she had a right to be in that bedroom alone with her lover if she chose. There was a TV in the living room so they did not need to come into her bedroom to watch TV. Besides Tammy needed her rest, and with these women barging in and out Tammy never got any rest.

I asked Tammy if she had ever told these women that her bedroom was off limits. She said that it had never occurred to her. So I asked Tammy if she would be willing to hold a meeting and tell them that from this day forward the only person allowed in her bedroom was her lover Chris.

Tammy thought about it for several minutes. Then she said that she could call a meeting. Chris was her lover and as such should really be the only other person in there. She really did need her rest. Chris grinned from ear to ear. I got Tammy to agree to a time for the meeting and her business word that she would follow through.

The next week Chris arrived by herself. She reported that the meeting had gone extremely well. Everyone agreed. Tammy's bedroom was off limits to everyone but Chris. Naturally Chris could be there because she was Tammy's lover. Chris reported that she now had some privacy and that Tammy was getting her rest. Chris then asked me if I would help her with some other problems. She had decided that I was OK since I had helped her and Tammy solve their problem.

Her history was filled with brutal physical abuse by her father. Her mother was a severe alcoholic. At 14, her father beat her for the last time; she left home. She was now 27 and had never gone back. Her brother was still home. He was a drug addict. Each time he got into difficulty his parents bailed him out. Chris hated her brother because as a kid he was never hit, only loved. That was the problem; she hated her brother.

I told Chris that I was sort of glad that her father had beat her because he had loved her enough to drive her away from that poisonous home. To stay there was to go crazy. I could tell that her brother was skillfully trapped at home. I would bet that not only did her brother do drugs to stay home, I would bet he acted really weird sometimes. She agreed that from time to time he tore his parents' home apart when he was freaked out on some drugs. I asked her to put herself in her brother's shoes for a moment. She could realize then that staying home was only possible if you were drunk, drugged or crazy. If she were home standing in her brother's shoes she would never have left. She would never have met her wonderful Tammy. She would never have become Tammy's lover. She would never have been able to help Tammy in all the many ways that were special to Tammy and made Chris feel worthwhile.

What she really needed to do was go home and shake her brother's hand. She really needed to thank him for being the family nut so she could leave and live a decent life. She also needed to shake her father's hand and thank him for brutalizing her so much that he drove her away at an early age. He must have loved her a lot to have figured out a way to get her out of that horrible home so she did not have to stay home and be the family nut like her brother.

Chris's eyes had become defocused as I talked. She sat quietly without moving for quite a while. She finally stirred a bit and asked me if I would run that by her again. So I did. She defocused again, sat quietly for an even longer period of time. She again shifted in her chair, refocused her eyes, then stretched.

"I've got to think about this stuff. I gotta go. See you next week." Having said that she got up from her chair and left the office. She canceled the following week but came in the next week. She told this amazing story of what she had done since I had talked to her.

She had gone to see her family. Her brother was even nuttier than I had described. So she went up to him and thanked him for being such a great nut. Any time he wanted to give it up he could because she was doing just fine and didn't need his help anymore. She then went to her father. She reported that she shook his hand and thanked him for beating her into leaving. She told him that she now understood that it was the only way she could have left. She also told him she knew that he loved her very much to do what he did. She said he mumbled some words and then asked her if she wanted to go fishing next weekend with him. He had missed his fishing buddy. The next weekend they went fishing.

While they were fishing from the dock her father got on her about being gay. Chris said that she had had it with all his shit. She put down her fishing pole and went over to her dad. She told him that she was going to live her life her way. To make sure he understood she said that she picked him up and pitched him into the lake.

He waded ashore cussing and swearing. By now she was laughing so hard she could hardly tell her story. He came out on the dock to get her. She told him to cut out all this shit or she would throw him in again and again until he got it into his thick head that she was grown up, living a decent life, and he could not do that to her anymore. He swung at her, she ducked, came up under him, picked him up again and threw him back into the lake. She told me at this point that she is about four inches taller than him. She is all muscles and he is an old goat with a beer belly. He waded ashore again and came after her a third time, again landing in the lake. This time he said he had enough of the lake and offered to make peace. She said that she went up and shook hands with her dad. They stopped fishing for a while and built a fire so he could dry out. From then on she reported they got along just great.

I started to comment on her delightfully successful story when she jumped up. She went out of the office and out the front door. I hardly had time to wonder what was going on when she came back to the office. She stomped up to me with two pink carnations held in her outstretched hand. "Here," she said, "these are for you. For such a scared little chicken you do OK as a shrink." She slapped me a couple of times on my back as she talked. "One of these carnations is for Patti, your lover. I don't want her getting any wrong ideas. Thanks for your help. See you around."

Potent Memories

This case illustrates the importance of accepting clients within their own framework. If the viability of this client's lifestyle had not been accepted I do not believe therapy would have been helpful. This was a man who took great pride in his ability to care for himself. Hypnosis was a wonderful tool to allow him the full satisfaction of working out the problem himself. "Suggestion merely arranges circumstances and choices so that natural mental mechanisms (that are usually processed in an unconscious manner) are made available for creative and therapeutic purposes" (Erickson, 1985, p. 17). "The unconscious mind is the storehouse for all personality experiences, personality learnings and personality attitudes" (Erickson, 1985, p. 2).

Scott was a 29-year-old man who had an athletic look of physical fitness. He was tan, muscular, with a graceful balanced walk and a wonderful smile that created some wrinkles around his eyes. His problem began when he moved to the Northwest two years ago. At first he thought the problem was related to the stress of moving, a new job, meeting new people in every area of his life. He said that he now felt settled in and had adjusted well to living in the Northwest. However, his problem persisted. He had tried everything he could think of to fix this problem but nothing had worked. The reason it was a BIG problem now was that he had met a wonderful man and had fallen in love. He wiggled about in his chair, looked down at his feet, cleared his throat, started to say something, and lapsed into silence.

"Well, Scott," I said, "Keeping up...with new terminology in the gay world has always been a problem for me. It seems like the harder I try, the harder I wish I could remember a new definition, the more apt it is to stay down...hidden in the inner recesses of my mind. If I could just say it to someone else soon then the problem would resolve itself. So I am going to burden you with this new definition I learned today. I suppose you knew that straight women that hang around gay men are called 'fag hags'?"

He looked at me and said, "Yes, I know that."

"Did you also know they were called 'fruit flies'?"

With that we both laughed until tears came to our eyes. He started to talk again and laughed instead. He finally collected himself. "Well," he said, "I can't get it up. I have been impotent since I moved to the Northwest. I work out, I eat right, I never in my whole life have had this problem. I even had a physical to see if there was something really wrong with me. The doctor said I was in perfect shape. There was nothing wrong with me. I have never been in therapy before. I always just kind of work things out in my mind. This time I can't seem to work it out."

Scott again lapsed into silence. I decided that it would be a good time to get a brief history of his growing up years and how he had lived his life up to this point. Scott grew up in a small rural Midwestern town. Everyone in his family worked hard. His parents were religious but did not expect their children to follow exactly in their footsteps when it came to religion. He reported that he knew he was gay when he was just a boy. After graduating from high school he knew that he had to get away from that small rural environment. With his parents' blessing he moved to a large Midwestern city. He found employment, met many gay men, and felt "at home" for the first time in his life. He fell in love with a wonderful man and lived with that man until he moved to the Northwest.

When Scott got to this last part he began to cry. He said that he loved this man very much. In fact he would always love him but he was not able to live with him. It was painful leaving his lover. His adjustment to the Northwest had been slow. He had initially dated infrequently but as the months moved along so did dating. He had met another man earlier but had not kept it up, because he was afraid if he did he would forget all the wonderful memories of his "true love." Now he knew if he failed to keep up his love with this new man he would lose him too. He said that he felt trapped. He very much wanted to keep up with his memories and his new love.

I told Scott that in this case I believed that hypnosis would solve his problems of trying to keep up…memories and keep up…a new lover. Scott said he was willing to try anything. If I felt that hypnosis would help, he would try hypnosis. The rest of the session was spent helping him discover his ability to utilize hypnosis for relaxing, dreaming, for catalepsy of his arm, for heating and cooling different parts of his body. He enjoyed discovering his talent to do things with his body that he had not thought possible.

He was given a homework assignment. He was to spend all the time he needed to round up all those important memories that he had of his "true love" and that the back of his mind would help him think of all he needed to know between this session and the next. He was encouraged to practice once or twice a day, utilizing his talents, see if he could become more skilled at doing with his body what he once thought was impossible, such as warming and cooling different parts of his body.

A week later at his next appointment, Scott reported that he had practiced twice a day and really enjoyed the time. He said that he had carefully gone over all the hours, days, weeks and years that he and his lover had spent together. It really helped to do it in trance. Somehow in trance he seemed to have all the time he needed to review carefully all those important memories.

I congratulated him on having practiced so diligently, for I knew how important it was to keep up...with those difficult memories. I suggested that since he now knew how to go into a comfortable trance he could use this session to continue learning what he wanted to learn. Scott said that he was ready to continue and settled into a trance without additional assistance from me.

"Now Scott, you have spent time this week reviewing all those impotent memories. With one part of your mind I want you to continue that review to make sure that you have included all those memories. As you do that with one part of your mind I am going to ask another part of your mind to decide if your right arm or your left arm will lift up to your cheek. Your conscious mind can guess which arm will lift and your unconscious mind can have the full satisfaction of agreeing or disagreeing. But you really don't know how that problem will be resolved, but you do know hot and cold, in and out, up and down. Now, I would like another part of your mind to heat or cool the arm that lifts. Or perhaps you would like cool cheeks and a throbbing hot arm. That's right. Lifting without thinking.

"As you review those memories I would like you to discover within your mind a safe place to store all those wonderful memories. Take all the time you need to really look. This memory bank can only be located by you. You are the only one who can ever know where this memory bank is located. You may need to make a key to unlock this memory bank and you may need to return to it many times to be sure you can locate it under any circumstance. That's right, that hand can continue to drift up and when it reaches that comfortable familiar place it can stay there a while, can it not? Have you located your memory bank?" Scott nodded yes.

"Now Scott, it is utterly important that you can locate this place under any and all conditions. So take all the time you need to arrange all the situations you know of that could get you lost, so you could not locate this place. For this is the storehouse of impotent memories. When you are sure, really sure, then place all those wonderful important memories there. When you have done that to your total satisfaction, stored all those impotent memories, lock up and leave. Don't go too far...just far enough, then come back, open the storehouse and see if all the impotent memories are really there. Any time that you have additional important memories to put there you can. You can always return, reopen that memory safe and add the impotent memories to all those others. Any time you wish you can quickly and easily return to review at your leisure all those important memories. As you said in trance you have all the time you need to accomplish that important review.

"The pleasure of knowing to your total satisfaction what your body can do without any effort. You have become fully absorbed in the task at hand. The pleasure and delight of learning again that your body, without thinking, can heat and cool effortlessly, fully, that extension of yourself.

"Now, Scott, when you have placed all those wonderful memories of your 'true love' in your memory bank and know that nothing can deflect your path, your arm will return to your lap. You might enjoy awaking with a sensation of comfortable warmth in your hands or your face. Take all the time you need to really learn all that you came here to remember. The back of your mind knows what you have learned and it goes with you. You can awaken remembering consciously that which will satisfy your conscious mind, and the rest will be there effortlessly, naturally in the back of your mind to come up at the right time in the future."

Scott spent about 15 minutes more in trance. When he reoriented he said, "Boy, I really feel spent but totally relaxed!"

"That's right. The pleasure of feeling spent, limp from pleasurable effort without even knowing you are..."

I quickly shifted the focus away by saying that I had another definition and needed to fix it in my mind. I said, "Straight is hanging up on an obscene phone call and Gay is making the obscene phone caller hang up." Scott gave a smile and agreed that maybe it was a joke I could forget.

Scott called two days before the next appointment, which had been scheduled for three weeks away. He did not need to come in. He no longer had a problem. He related that he couldn't remember what we did but somehow to his great delight he was his old self.

I bumped into Scott at a party two years later. He thought I looked vaguely familiar. Had we met? He introduced himself and his lover of two years. They both looked very comfortable together, that special togetherness that love creates.

Conclusion

I must confess that being gay has skewed my basic needs. Most people talk about wanting to be happy, to be loved, as the most important thing in their lives. They often come into therapy saying that is what they want: to be loved, to be happy. If they could be loved, be happy, then their life would be perfect. What many gays hunger for is acceptance. What I hunger for is legitimization. That is why this "lavender duster" struggles to be the best Ericksonian therapist possible. Milton Erickson's whole being, it seems to me, focused on ways to overcome our limited understanding of what it means to be human. To me, this is the magic of Milton Erickson. As a gay woman I cannot begin to describe the joy, the relief, the hope that grew within me as I studied Erickson's works. I periodically entertain the fantasy that some day, some time in the future, all people who work in this field of mental health will have incorporated Erickson's basic philosophy and made it their own. To be a practitioner is to be open to understanding human behavior in all its magnificent variety.

References

Erickson, M. H. (1980). *The collected papers of Milton H. Erickson on hypnosis, Vol. 4. Innovative hypnotherapy* (E. L. Rossi, Ed.). New York: Irvington.

Erickson, M. H. (1985). *Life reframing in hypnosis: The seminars, workshops, and lectures of Milton H. Erickson* (Vol. 2, E. L. Rossi, M. O. Ryan, & F. A. Sharp, Eds.). New York: Irvington.

Havens, R. (1985). *The wisdom of Milton H. Erickson*. New York: Irvington.

The Application of Ericksonian Approaches to Autistic Children

Keiichi Miyata, M.A.

*Keiichi Miyata, M.A. (Kyushu University) is an Associate Professor in the De-
partment of Education at Niigata University in Japan. He translated into Japanese*
A Teaching Seminar with Milton Erickson *(J. Zeig, Ed., Brunner/Mazel, 1980).*

*Miyata presents the treatment used with two difficult cases. He emphasizes a
utilization approach which gains rapport through the use of focal symptomatic behaviors. Since his practice is in Japan, this article provides a fascinating cultural perspective regarding Ericksonian work.*

Niigata University's Department of Education has a child guidance
center which treats autistic conditions and other less severe emotional
problems. For the past five years we have been using an Ericksonian
approach in the treatment of clients. This chapter presents two cases where
Erickson's utilization technique was used to alter the behavior of autistic
children.

Although we do not use direct hypnosis for improving symptomatic
behavior of handicapped, intellectually impaired children, we do employ
Erickson's utilization techniques with these children. For example, one of
our teachers redirected the bizarre finger movements of an autistic child to
piano playing. In another case, a child who was obsessed with getting
good scores on everything refused to drink milk. The teacher utilized the
child's obsession to change behavior by giving him high points every time
he drank milk.

Erickson used this strategic approach in the treatment of mentally retarded patients and in the field of rehabilitation. There was one case of

The author thanks his graduate student, Kazue Izumi and research students,
Masahiro Otaki and Kisaburo Hoshino for their help in preparing this article, and
is grateful to Sally Franek, Ph.D., for her assistance in correcting a draft of this
article.

Address reprint requests to Keiichi Miyata, Niigata University, Faculty of Education, 8050, Ikarashi Ni-No-Cho, Niigata-Shi, Japan 950-21.

family therapy which included a 20-year-old mentally retarded girl who had temper tantrums. Erickson advised the therapist, "The thing to do is to get your patient, any way you wish, any way you can, to do something." This girl's energy was rechanneled into making a stuffed purple cow (Zeig, 1980). Erickson similarly treated a brain-damaged patient with severe aphasia, alexia, and a thalamic syndrome using hypnotically oriented psychotherapy (Erickson, 1963). In a third case he used a strategic mode to treat a patient who had suffered a stroke, utilizing the patient's Prussian character to do so (Haley, 1973).

Employing strategic interventions, we consider the patient's social context, especially the familial environment. Before proceeding further, I would like to discuss some characteristics common to Japanese families that will be relevant to this assessment. Although declining somewhat, three-generation households made up almost half of all households in 1981 (Nasu, 1983). Further, almost 70 percent of adults over 65 years of age live with their children. Hence, compared to the United States, where many elderly couples maintain separate households, the influence of grandparents on the family is more direct. The intervention of grandmothers often causes problems between the grandmother and the daughter-in-law.

Case Reports

Case 1

An eight-year-old boy was brought to our guidance room by his mother because of his habit of making bizarre bilateral hand movements in front of his face. The problem developed at age three. His family consisted of his parents, his younger brother, and his grandmother on his father's side. His parents owned and operated a liquor store.

The child could understand almost everything that was said to him and was capable of making three-word sentences. Occasionally he manifested echolalia and the use of random words. He attended all his classes at the same school; half were for normal children and the other half were for emotionally disturbed children. Except for problems with schoolwork and the hand movements, he was well adjusted socially and liked by his schoolmates. He and his younger brother related well.

We employed passive play therapy with the child to observe his behavior. The main part of our therapy was an independently conducted interview with his mother, who seemed overconcerned about his behavior. The bizarre hand movements occurred when the boy was happy, when his mother refused his demands, and when he was alone. His mother, however, could not give us a detailed picture of when the behavior occurred. When she shouted at him to stop, he would do so. The hand movements would restart a few minutes later. When this behavior was most persistent, she would try to stop him by grabbing his hands.

His favorite activities were taking walks, watching trains at railway crossings, and being chased. He also liked to stock the cigarette vending machine in front of the family shop. When he put the packets into the top of the machine and heard the sound of them falling through to the bottom, he was overjoyed and produced the bizarre hand movements in front of his face. He also had a habit of exaggerating and lying. For example, he would hold up a pack of "High Light" cigarettes and purposely say these were "Mild Seven." The same pattern occurred concerning the names of banks and he would reject his mother's corrections. However, if she recognized what he said as being true, he would show surprise.

The mother appeared to be bright and cheerful, but doubted the usefulness of our conducting an interview with her. Because of her knowledge of autism she was concerned about the theoretical position of the therapist. When questioned, the therapist gave her an intentionally vague answer, which caused her to clarify her own beliefs. She believed that his autism was caused by the shock of not wearing warm clothing during the winter when he was two years old.

We could see that the boy's behavior was at least partially influenced by his mother's attitude. When she was calm and relaxed, the frequency of his behavior decreased. Her major approach in dealing with the child focused on stopping the hand movements, sometimes using threats.

Therapy proceeded cautiously; the therapist did not give her a definite direction for about one month. By that time, she was concerned about what to do with his behavior. She described herself as "impatient." Given her frustration with the situation, we decided that the time was right for therapeutic directives to be accepted without resistance. The following directive was given:

"If you went to a doctor for treatment, you would follow his advice fully. We want you to take the same attitude toward us. When your son's behavior occurs, we would like you to imitate him in an amplified manner in front of him. You should continue until he says something. By doing so, you will be able to understand the situation, the strength of his behavior, and how he feels while he moves his hands."

After the first week, she reported that her son's problematic behavior had stopped. This was confirmed by his grandmother. Mother rationalized the change in her son's behavior. She indicated that the first week was unusual and saw no connection between the change in the boy's behavior and her actions. When she imitated his behavior, he verbalized using the words, "go," or "Mum, go" or his friend's name. The word "go" means "go away" in this case. She thought he used his friend's name because he liked the friend's mother who was a kind woman.

A week later, she reported being unconcerned about his behavior, even though it reappeared about five times a day. She described the times she spent with the boy. She had only about four hours a day to be with him and during that time her interactions were halfhearted. Housekeeping and the family business occupied her time. She was concerned about her husband's relationship with the boy. Her husband often showed anger toward his son. Although, she had never proposed it, she wanted her husband to be positively involved with their son. Also, her life was made more difficult by the grandmother who was a good woman, but a fussy eater and difficult to care for.

The mother frequently failed to comply with our directives. Instead, she used her former method of behavioral suppression. As a punishment, we directed her to go for an evening walk with her son and the dog for exactly 30 minutes. We told her to inform her husband and the grandmother about this directive in order to obtain their full cooperation. Two weeks later, she reported to us how she had felt during these walks. She realized her son was anxious, and how his anxiety prompted much of his problematic behavior. She linked his behavior to her failure to follow through on promises. During the walks, the boy gained a needed sense of responsibility by taking the dog's lead.

The family was cooperative, although household duties sometimes kept the mother from taking the walks. She gradually established a new position in the family, one with more dominance. The grandmother's cooperation increased markedly. The mother became more assertive with her husband. For the first time, she asked him to stop being hostile with his son. The father began to show affection for the child, while previously it had seemed to the mother that he did not like the boy. Furthermore, she reported the hand movements were no longer noticeable and that she didn't worry about them any longer.

We interviewed her again two months after the school year began. During the vacation, the boy was with his brother at a camp for handicapped children. On his return home, his behavior temporarily worsened. Nonetheless, she reported that he had matured. He no longer needed to hold his mother's hand during walks with the dog, but instead followed her on his bicycle. For the first week after camp, she imitated his behavior. It took him a long time to verbalize his response. Gradually his condition improved to the point where he quickly stopped his movements and began to say, "I will not do it anymore." The therapist redirected the mother to imitate him in a caring and supportive fashion. She became concerned, however, that her son's behavior had worsened largely as a result of her imitations. She was concerned that there was something wrong with her attitude toward him.

Two weeks later, during the twelfth session, the therapist felt that the mother's communication with the boy had changed. She reported that when he spoke to her she listened and replied in a composed manner. He stopped his oppositional behavior. She also learned that keeping him company had the positive effect of decreasing his bizarre hand movements. The boy came to realize that if he produced the hand movements, his mother would imitate him. He would pretend, with a smile, to start the movement to test her attitude or he would move his hand in front of his face at first and then change, suddenly putting his hands on his head. Thus, he came to make fun of his mother. While not wanting to report her feelings, she admitted to us that she had spontaneously realized the meaning of the imitation. Although she had felt that she was an open person, it had been difficult for her to imitate him in front of other people. She realized how much she had been concerned with keeping up her own appearance, and that it was useless to think only of trying to stop the boy's hand movement. The therapist accepted her insight into the need to discard her concern with keeping up her own appearance.

Two months later, during the fifteenth session, she reported that there was still a little hand movement, but it did not worry her. She also reported that at school the teacher no longer noticed it. Therefore, she had ceased to imitate him. She confessed to us that once or twice a day she had found herself in a situation where she could not imitate him because of concern about her own appearance. The walks had also become less frequent, because the boy told her not to go with him as he would rather ride his bicycle alone.

One-and-a-half months later, she reported that the frequency of his hand movements had stabilized to the point where she hardly noticed them. Her communication with him was gradually improving and her response to him was much better. The boy also began to converse properly and sensibly. Therapy was terminated after nine months.

One-and-a-half years later, he continues to control his hand movements, even though on occasion his hands stop in front of his face when he is thinking of something. Our major intervention was to teach the mother how to communicate with her son. The mother had been worried about her son's bizarre pattern of hand movement. We utilized her overconcern and the boy's humorous pattern of intentionally saying something opposite or different and suggested to her that she should communicate with him through imitation.

We understood that his unique behavior patterns showed unconscious needs to communicate, because these kinds of symptomatic behavior are considered a social function. By having his own behavior patterns utilized in a slightly modified manner, we expected the child to become confused and cease his behavior. Furthermore, through the mother's imitation, the boy had to confront a mirror image of himself.

As for the mother, her mental set was always passive and focused on his behavior. Our paradoxical directive prompted her to be more active by making her watch for the boy's behavior to begin. Her previous communication with the boy had been halfhearted and concerned with inhibiting him. Through the task of walking with him, she was able to establish communication and consequently established her position in the family— gaining her own free time and the cooperation of her family. That task was strategically presented as a punishment, the mother not fully realizing its meaning. In carrying out this task, the mother provoked a reorganization of the family system.

We attempted to place her in a therapeutic double-bind. If her imitation of the boy's behavior decreased his bizarre movements, it proved that her attitude was the problem. On the other hand, if she resisted our directives, the boy's behavior would remain the same. In order to relieve this double-bind, her only alternative was to decrease the boy's anxiety through increased contact and communication. The therapist's goal was to modify the mother-child relationship by reframing aspects of their communication. We do not understand the reason for the persistent bizarre behavior of autistic children, but this case illustrates that there is the possibility for change.

Case 2

The client in this case was an autistic junior high school boy in eighth grade who was brought to us by his mother. His family consisted of his parents and his younger brother. He had a variety of symptoms including a habit of crying loudly or groaning both at home and at school without any apparent reason. While groaning, he would grasp the windowsill and, pivoting on his hands, would move backwards and forwards in a swinging motion. His mother described it as similar to rowing a boat. He would also attach pieces of Scotch-tape on certain parts of his body. In addition, he had a habit of taking a stick in each hand and waving them for awhile before breaking them. He would also cause lacerations and scabs by biting his right hand.

He attained speech at age two. His early speech included "give me," and "mum." However, at the age of six he was only able to say short sentences such as "I go home," "I go bathroom."

His symptomatic behavior evolved over a series of years. It first became noticeable when he entered nursery school. At bedtime, he would lie on top of his favorite blanket, one with a picture of Bambi on it. He could not sleep without this ritual. This behavior persisted until the picture wore off two years later. His odd behavior involving sticks began when he was given an oblong block by his nursery school teacher to keep him calm. Later, his demands shifted to pencils, ice-cream sticks, and a variety of sticks at home. At nursery school, he started his habit of biting the heel of his right hand. Instances of his swinging his body on the window sill while groaning increased during the fifth grade.

After entering junior high school, he became obsessed with the feeling of his tight fitting school cap and would wear it at home and at school, refusing to remove it during lessons. Five months later, his cap became so unsanitary that he had no choice but to discard it. At the same time, he started wearing cloth gloves. His mother always had a new pair of gloves for him, which he wore for one year. His groaning became so noisy during school that his teacher covered his mouth with packing tape. The boy seemed to like the feeling of the tape and demanded it be placed on his cheeks instead of his mouth. His mother was embarrassed by the big brown tape on his face, and decided to replace it with smaller pieces of white tape at home. Then the boy came to want tape on all his fingers. Since then, he had stopped wearing the gloves.

The boy put the tape on his face, on his fingers, and on the inside of his elbows. He compulsively positioned the tape, and when it would come off due to perspiration, he would demand more. His mother would give him tape to take to school. He would hold out his arms in a rigid position so that the tape on his arms would stick properly.

He invariably positioned the tape on his fingers just in front of the second finger joint. No other position was tolerated. The tape on his arms began to irritate his skin, so his mother temporarily satisfied his demand with handkerchiefs. He kept the tape stuck to his cheeks, his arms and his index fingers for two months. His mother confessed that she was sometimes so irritated by his continual crying and groaning that she wanted to kill him.

Since the tape on each cheek was still large enough to cause the mother significant embarrassment, she asked us to do something about it. Hence, we focused our therapy on his use of the tape. In order to develop rapport with him, however, we treated another symptomatic behavior first. In our play room, the boy picked up a pair of drum sticks and waved them in a vertical motion. The therapist imitated him at first and then took the lead in rhythm by waving some sticks horizontally. At this, the boy shouted "no, no" and stopped waving the sticks. In the play room, there was a low shelf for toys. He used this to swing his body as he had been doing on the window sill both at home and school. When it looked as if he were going to start this behavior, the therapist intervened and directed him to do 20 sit-ups. The boy said "no" but complied with the therapist's directive. Due to these interventions, the boy's habit of waving sticks and swinging his body disappeared during therapy by the sixth session. We then concentrated our attention on his use of the tape.

When his bands became dirty, we directed him to wash them. Naturally the tape became wet, so we had him remove it. The therapist helped him take the tape off and replaced it with Band-Aids on each of his little fingers. If the therapist put the tape on the end of his fingers, he shouted loudly, but if the tape were put just in front of the second joint, he remained calm. Tape on only his little fingers was not enough and he demanded that his other fingers be taped. He became so irritated he put his hand in his pants touching his buttocks and scratched his head.

We told him to wash his hands again and then replaced the Band-Aids on his little fingers. This was repeated several times, taking more and more time to communicate with him about the tape and gradually making him wait longer and longer before we changed the Band-Aids. As a result, the boy stopped demanding tape on all his fingers. We told him that only the therapist was allowed to change the tape, which he accepted. Consequently he appeared happy to come to the therapy sessions.

When he arrived at the next session, we found Scotch tape on his cheeks, handkerchiefs tied around his elbows, and Scotch tape on his index fingers. We shifted the position of the tape on his index fingers from just in front of the second joints to the ends of his fingers and replaced the tape with Band-Aids. When the therapist tried to touch the handkerchiefs around his elbows, he shouted "no," groaned, and rejected the therapist's approach. We employed the same intervention for the tape on his cheeks. Asking him to wash his face, we gradually made the pieces smaller and shifted the position to a little below that of the original placement. Because of this, the boy began to groan. We then repeated the intervention of having him wash his face and again shifted the position of the new Band-Aids.

When he arrived for the next session, we found the tape placed in the original locations. During the session we used the dirtiness associated with the tape as a rationale for washing his fingers and moving the tape to the finger tips. We tried to replace the handkerchiefs with small Band-Aids, but each time he groaned and refused. We let the handkerchiefs remain. The large pieces of tape on his face were replaced with small pieces just below the original positions. We slowly and carefully did this twice. The boy, however, became impatient and began to inflict self-injury by biting the heel of his right hand. We utilized his poor coordination, saying "no, that is the wrong hand," whereupon he would try to put his left hand to his mouth, which he found difficult. We let him see the Band-Aids on his face by looking into the mirror, at which point we ended the session.

When the boy returned home, he demanded that the small pieces of Band-Aid be replaced with larger ones. He was insistent and his mother complied. He did not, however, demand any tape for his fingers, and allowed the handkerchiefs on his elbows to be replaced with pieces of tape. This may have been because it was now autumn and he had started wearing long sleeve shirts but we were now seeing even more progress.

At the start of next session, we again replaced the large pieces of tape on his cheeks with small ones. The therapist made him confirm there were two pieces by making him count them. He was able to count, but did not understand the concept of any number above two. Next, we took the tape off his arms and put one small piece back over the mole just below the inside of his left arm. Then we made him wash his face and replaced only one Band-Aid on his right cheek. By making him count cross-laterally from his right cheek to his left elbow and utilizing the resulting confusion, we helped him to confirm that there were two pieces.

When the boy arrived for the tenth session, there were two small pieces of Band-Aid on his cheeks. There was no tape on either arm. It had taken six months to reach this stage. We tried to remove the pieces on his cheeks and replace them with one piece on his jaw. He again objected so we shifted one piece back to his right cheek. When he demanded a Band-Aid for his left cheek, we asked him to attach it by himself. Even though he exclaimed, "no, no," he complied.

At the next two sessions, the boy arrived with a small piece of Band-Aid on his right cheek. He came to the thirteenth session without tape on his face and was unaware of the missing tape. Both at home and during the therapy, when he realized the tape was missing, he would demand it in a quiet voice only, and he was given just one small piece. He had also ceased demanding tape in other locations. Furthermore, we observed during therapy that if a Band-Aid was put onto the heel of his right hand, he would not bite it. Therapy terminated at this point, having lasted eight months.

For the next six months, the boy was satisfied with one small piece of tape which was hardly noticeable. He remained stable. Currently, his behaviors of biting his hand and swinging his body on the windowsill are not fully controlled, but occur very infrequently.

Our strategy with the family was to gain the father's cooperation and get him involved in the son's problem by taking his son for walks, to the pool, and cycling during the summer vacation. We met the parents at the fifth session prior to the vacation and gave the father our directive, which was also aimed at rechanneling the boy's energy. We also interviewed the school teacher who had no effective means of dealing with the boy and had wanted him transferred to a special school. During this interview we learned of his surprise that the boy no longer demanded tape. We described the utilization approach as a treatment model, which paradoxically directed the teacher not to inhibit his behavior. This helped us to gain the teacher's understanding and cooperation.

We treated this child by utilizing his symptoms. In order to begin moving the tape, we utilized the facial dirt collected by the tape, and his muscular tension. He suffered from tension in his shoulder and upper back, and the therapist made him lie on his stomach and gently massaged his body to relieve the tension. He was very pleased with this treatment and began to ask the therapist for it spontaneously. Through this strategy, his face became so dirty that we could then make him wash his face and replace the tape. Thus, we communicated with him through body contact nonverbally and through the topic of tape verbally. The water also had the meaning, metaphorically, of washing out the inner pain of his heart. We changed the size and position of the tape according to Erickson's technique of symptom substitution (Erickson, 1954). We were able to bring the boy to a point where he needed only one piece, utilizing his ability to grasp the numerical concept of two. We also reduced his groaning by giving him the ordeal of doing sit-ups.

The instances of self-injury had not been numerous, but when they occurred, we were able to change them by utilizing his lack of coordination and making him try to bite his left hand. At the eighth session, his mother informed us that by the same technique, she had been able to make him stop this self-injury.

It can be that his need for tape was based not only on seeking a stimulus on a sensory level, but also a sense of security and self-protection on an inner level. By metaphorically using Band-Aids we were able to respect the boy's apparent need for security and self-protection, and at the same time decrease the number of pieces to one while repeatedly shifting the position. He could not understand the metaphorical meaning of Band-Aids, but understood experientially how they were used. We believe that for him, the remaining one Band-Aid is necessary to satisfy his sense of security and self-protection. Because of this, and the rare recurrence of his palm biting behavior, we are planning further therapy and devising a new strategy to channel his energy.

Conclusion

Milton Erickson's utilization approach was used in the treatment of two autistic children. Handicapped children often display several dysfunctional behaviors, hence, treatment approaches that use the client's existing behavior will be effective in producing change. Our interventions took into account each child's unique character and symptomatic behaviors. This individualized approach is an essential aspect of any Ericksonian intervention.

Our work has important implications for other client populations. For example, therapy can be designed to assist brain-injured patients to retrieve and utilize their own resources. We would like to urge other therapists to experiment with Ericksonian techniques in a variety of clinical settings. Through this expansion, new facets of Milton Erickson's work will be discovered.

References

Erickson, M. H. (1954). Special techniques of brief hypnotherapy. *Journal of Clinical and Experimental Hypnosis, 2,* 109–129.

Erickson, M. H. (1963). Hypnotically oriented psychotherapy in organic brain damage. *The American Journal of Clinical Hypnosis, 6,* 92–112.

Haley, J. (1973). *Uncommon therapy.* New York: Norton.

Nasu, S. (1983). Old people and family. In K. Morioka (Ed.), *Family sociology* (pp. 118–119). Tokyo: Yuhikaku (in Japanese).

Zeig, J. K. (Ed.) (1980). *A teaching seminar with Milton H. Erickson.* New York: Brunner/Mazel.

"Dangerous to Self and Others": The Management of Acute Psychosis Using Ericksonian Techniques of Hypnosis and Hypnotherapy

John H. Edgette, Psy.D.

John H. Edgette, Psy.D. (Hahnemann University) is a clinical psychologist in private practice and Director of The Milton H. Erickson Institute of Philadelphia. He authored a chapter on Ericksonian therapy with agoraphobics in Ericksonian Psychotherapy *(Zeig, 1985).*

Edgette shows how several agitated psychotics were hypnotized using an Ericksonian approach. His inductions were bold attempts to introduce hypnosis in a setting where drugs and restraints are often the only available tools. He offers some ideas concerning the myth that hypnosis will not work with such a population.

Emergency rooms and crisis intervention units commonly accept psychotic and agitated patients off the streets. These patients often present an immediate management problem and can be extremely dangerous to themselves and to others. There is a risk that staff and other patients can become seriously injured by an agitated psychotic patient. In long-term units and day treatment programs patients can become unstable and present similar problems.

It is a commonly held belief that medicating these patients in times of extreme agitation will bring an end to the difficulties. However, even when medication is available, there are often delays until it can be administered and still other delays until its effects begin to stabilize the patient. Sometimes, of course, medication doesn't work, and sometimes it cannot

---

Address reprint requests to John H. Edgette, Psy. D., The Milton H. Erickson Institute of Philadelphia, Suite 8, 1062 Lancaster Ave., Rosemont, PA 19010.

be given at all due to contraindications. Danger and disturbance persist in these settings and techniques are needed for helping these patients. Hypnosis can be helpful in meeting this need.

Hypnosis has traditionally been seen as either difficult or therapeutically detrimental when used with psychotic patients. Despite a lack of hard evidence, a number of reasons for this position have been cited: 1) since the patients' attentional capacities were greatly diminished, they would not be able to focus and concentrate as needed, precluding trance; 2) the trance state would direct patients inward and their reality contact would suffer further; and 3) hypnotic work would, by necessity, foster even greater regression (Scagnelli-Jobsis, 1982).

A review of the literature (Scagnelli-Jobsis, 1982) systematically elucidates that each of these assertions are unfounded both clinically and experimentally. The Ericksonian perspective espoused in this article will go even further to show how poor attention span, lowered reality contact, and regression can actually be used to effect trance and increase appropriate behavior (Erickson, 1980). The emphasis is on a utilization approach, reframing and siding with the resistance (Erickson, 1964).

Pacing and Leading Attention

The diminished attentional abilities of the psychotic patient pose great problems for the traditionally "authoritarian" hypnotist since concentration on the therapists' preselected medium for purposes of induction is often impossible. Gilligan (1982) bypassed the apparent resistance often encountered in attempting to secure the psychotic patient's attention by using the patient's hallucinations to begin trance induction. He used formal hypnosis to help a chronic schizophrenic gradually cease hallucinating visual images that were bizarre and gory. Gilligan began by having the patient hallucinate but in a relaxed state. He then had him hallucinate different images — comforting images. Finally, the patient stopped hallucinating altogether.

In this example, the keys to Gilligan's work were *pacing* the patient and *leading* him to different experiences. *Pacing* entails noting, actively accepting, and mimicking the subject's behavior to develop rapport. Using pacing, patients need not manifest any ability to concentrate. Therapists can monitor and pace whatever it is that the psychotic patient is focusing upon, shifting as rapidly as needed. In effect, one can side with the pathology to overcome the pathology. This position, once established, can become the point from which the hypnotist makes *leading* suggestions for different behavior. Further emphasis on pacing and leading with Ericksonian hypnosis and psychotic patients can be found in Dolan (1985).

Using pacing and leading, therapists can also capitalize on other processes that are characteristic of ego disintegration in addition to attentional
deficits, for example, regression and impaired reality testing.

The Controversy Over Hypnotizability

There is debate in the field concerning the *extent* to which patients
suffering from psychosis can be hypnotized. The Scagnelli-Jobsis (1982)
review concludes that psychotic patients are hypnotizable and may be
even more hypnotizable than other patient populations. However, Spiegel
(1983) has contested the accuracy of this review and its conclusions. He
calls attention to other studies not cited by Scagnelli-Jobsis, particularly
those using standardized scales of hypnotizability.

Perhaps the discrepant research findings can be reconciled by considering the flexible approach to induction inherent in the Ericksonian method.
Since attentional problems make psychotic people difficult to hypnotize,
we would *expect* experiments that use standard and authoritarian inductions to produce reduced hypnotic responsivity. Holding the independent
variable of the induction method and wording constant would naturally
result in poorer scores on suggestibility scales such as Spiegel's. Ericksonian strategies, relying upon pacing and leading, would enable inductions to be tailored to patients regardless of limits on their attention. This
would allow for deeper trance regardless of attentional capacities. The
discrepant research results cited may be a function of induction style
interacting with the variable capacity for concentration among "normals,"
neurotics, and psychotics. Hence, while Spiegel (1983) recommends re-
solving the apparent conflict in findings by more research using standard
suggestibility scales and better diagnosis, perhaps varying the *method* of
induction might prove more profitable. Psychotic patients may not be less
hypnotizable; they may merely need special modifications of technique.

An induction with wording that does not vary may be precise and
reduce error variance, but it will not show psychotic patients to be as
suggestible as they may well be. Perhaps it is no wonder then that research
that uses standardized inductions and performance scales shows that psychotics are less suggestible. On the other hand, research that uses the case
study method and naturalistic, informal and permissive Ericksonian induction strategies finds psychotics highly suggestible. Zeig (1974),
Erickson (1980), Erickson and Rossi (1980), and Dolan (1985) all think that
psychotics are highly responsive to suggestion, perhaps more so than even
most "normals." Again, this discrepancy in the literature can be resolved
by understanding that psychotics' fleeting attentional capacity does not
make them poor hypnotic subjects, but it does make them poor responders

to standardized inductions. Studies that have used a standardized induction for purposes of experimental rigor may be guilty of the classic mistake of their results being a product of their experimental methodology alone, not an understanding of objective reality.

Experimental concerns aside, this article will further help to resolve the clinical controversy by showing that an Ericksonian approach can induce trance in even the most disorganized population—psychotic patients who are actively agitated, hallucinating, delusional and dangerous. Erickson (1964, 1965, 1980), Erickson and Rossi (1980), Erickson and Zeig (1980), Zeig (1974), and Dolan (1985) have used similar techniques with psychotic patients. The emphasis in the following cases, however, is on patients who might be considered somewhat more uncooperative and dangerous at the time of the actual induction. Three cases will be used for illustration.

Case 1: Screaming Bobby

Bobby was a 22-year-old schizophrenic patient who was being put into four-point restraints after having hit a patient on the unit. The attack was unprovoked. Bobby's lability and disinhibition combined with his paranoia to make him volatile and unpredictable.

As he was being placed into restraints, Bobby still posed a great danger. Very strong, he was kicking, swinging and trying to bite staff members. He was in great psychic pain, as his primitive crying and endless ear-shattering screams evidenced. He was fearful and his eyes darted wildly around the room looking for the source of the voices.

The therapist slowly approached Bobby and said, "And you look quickly over there and there and there and here and there and up and down and over and out and then away over there, away, away, away. And while you look, you can listen closely to the soft sound of my voice and be surprised at the comfort that it gives you. And you can allow yourself to continue screaming as long and as loud as you like until you get it all out and it's over. And as this screaming comes to a slow end...winding down...you can gasp for air and recognize that there is a sudden sense of comfort, peace and silence inside. You can calm, calm, calm (softer), calm...calm and may even get sleepy, feeling safe and held." Variations of these suggestions were repeated for about three minutes. Amazingly, Bobby was actually asleep by the time the final restraint was fastened.

It is difficult to isolate the essential or definitive aspects of the induction that were crucial, but several components are noteworthy. First, his eye darting was accepted and paced, as was his screaming. The loss of ego boundaries commonly seen in psychosis makes it possible to rapidly join a patient by means of pacing. Further, the ego of the decompensating patient, often desperately seeking assistance, usually welcomes benevolent help. From this synchronous position, leading suggestions can be made. Here the author utilized the naturally occurring sense of reintegration and calm that everyone feels, even briefly, after a full scream. Bobby's great lability enabled that shift to be a profound experience for him. Deepening techniques sustained the sense of peace that he felt. As he was visibly exhausted, even sleep could be brought on.

Case 2: Bruce Lee

Reggie was a 32-year-old male patient diagnosed as suffering from manic-depressive psychosis. In his hypermanic states, he suffered from the delusion of being Bruce Lee, of cinematic martial arts fame. On a prior admission, Reggie had hit and seriously injured a worker. When the therapist initiated contact with him, he was pacing frantically, demanding that everyone recognize that he was Bruce Lee, and stating that he was ready to fight all staff members. Patients were scattering and staff attempts to help him were being ignored. Hospital security was called.

The therapist stayed a safe distance away, but said softly and slowly, "Mr. Lee? I've been hoping to meet you for a long time. I would like to study with you, to work with you. What I badly need to learn from you, great teacher, is the ancient Eastern art of self-control and relaxation. Let's go off to this quiet corner and I will tell you what I have heard you say in the past about inner calm." Beaming, but a bit baffled, Reggie gladly led the way to the designated area and sat down. The therapist continued, "I have heard you say, master, that first we close our eyes and breathe slowly and deeply and hold the breath for a moment and then gently and evenly exhale, feeling the breath for a moment and then gently and evenly inhale, feeling the breath move and feeling the calmness spread. I understand that it's important to…" The induction proceeded in a similar fashion for 15 more minutes.

Here, the patient's delusion was accepted, but he could maintain his grandiose position only if he allowed the therapist to define a new role behavior. Hence, being omnipotent and admired was contingent on permitting a reframing of what it meant to be Bruce Lee. During the induction, statements were phrased so that Reggie felt that he was doing the teaching at all times. Here, going "one down" resulted in the therapist gaining control and becoming "one up."

At the end of the session, Reggie gladly agreed to give "instruction" three times a day in the future. In return he would get food, lodging, and have access to all other unit services—including Lithium. Later in the day, the therapist aided his adjustment to a fearful, angry and unbelieving unit by telling Reggie, "You are the living embodiment of serene self-control. Patients and staff alike will be watching you to see this. But note that they are willful, proud, and stubborn, and they will never admit to learning from you. Family, friends and daily events may from time to time start to annoy you. These times will serve as small tests—people will look and learn in wonderment as you close your eyes, practice relaxation and remain calm."

Case 3: Bedtime Routines

Bill, a 24-year-old male patient, was grossly out of contact with reality. He was angry and agitated, moving out of control rapidly. Staff members had managed to get him to his room but they had been incapable of quieting him or helping him become self-contained. He received an injection of medicine but until it took effect he appeared dangerous and made numerous threats against staff. He was spontaneously, and wildly, jumping in and out of bed. When, finally, he was under the covers, the therapist used suggestion to try to bring on sleep. Each of Bill's bizarre movements were reframed as a necessary movement which was nonetheless, a precursor to deep, sound rest. For example, when the patient leapt up and pulled furiously at a locked closet door, the therapist responded, "And it is wise to check the front door to make sure it is locked before drifting off." After a few moments, the patient was out of bed again, using the bathroom. The therapist said, "Of course! Always pee before bed so that you don't have to get up again." Bill remained in bed and was quiet for five minutes but rocked vigorously and wildly on his back. This elicited, "Some people rock themselves to sleep." Bill was quiet for awhile but then screamed "Jesus" a few times. The therapist said, "Never forget to say your prayers before entering the land of safe, sweet, happy dreams." Together they then recited the Lord's prayer. At this point, the patient sighed deeply, curled up into a fetal position with his hand near his mouth, thumb extended. The therapist said, "And you may want to just move that thumb into your mouth...closer, closer it goes, oh, it would feel so good and safe and secure to suck on it...(after that the thumbsucking started) and you can perhaps remember a bedtime long ago when you felt warm and loved and everything was all right and you could easily fall into a deep, sound, calm sleep. A time when..."

In this example, direct and observable behaviors were paced, reframed and then used to potentiate a desired future response. The directed future behavior followed logically from the reframed meaning of what was happening. Yet, this does not always need to be true. With thought-disordered patients, the therapist has great freedom in connecting two events.

Acutely psychotic patients, abiding by the rules of primary process and not adhering to formal logic, tend not to fluster even if the leading suggestion has little to do with their current behavior. Poor reality contact seems to enable illogical leads to seem plausible. Often the linking statement "and now" is enough to make the connection, disrupt maladaptive behavior and redirect the patient into activities that will later result in enhanced reality contact.

A final point brought out in this case is that severe regression, while maladaptive on an everyday basis, can be utilized during trance to aid restabilization. Here the patient was successfully directed to a pleasant memory—almost everyone has at least a few pockets of residual happy recollections from childhood. In an already existing regressed condition these are more easily accessed.

Discussion

These case examples show that even floridly psychotic patients can be hypnotized via Ericksonian techniques. While creativity and flexibility is necessary, these patients can easily be induced into trance and can profit from the experience. None of the clinical fears and contraindications for using hypnosis with psychotic patients have been supported either here or elsewhere (Scagnelli-Jobsis, 1982). One reservation that continues to be reiterated is that "hypnosis is nearly impossible and trance induction is clinically contraindicated" with *uncooperative* or *angry* psychotic patients (Baker, 1983). In noting the differential effect of authoritarian standard inductions versus permissive and tailored inductions on the diminished attentional capacities of psychotic patients, this discrepancy in the research literature may be resolved. An Ericksonian approach, as exemplified in these cases, shows this resilient qualm to be unfounded. Ericksonian hypnotherapy can thus serve as a new alternative for the emergency room or crisis intervention center management of difficult and psychotic patients.

References

Baker, E. (1983). The use of hypnotic techniques with psychotics. *American Journal of Clinical Hypnosis, 25*, 283–288.

Dolan, Y. M. (1985). *A path with a heart.* New York: Brunner/Mazel.

Erickson, M. H. (1964). An hypnotic technique for resistant patients: The patient, the technique and its rationale and field experiments. *American Journal of Clinical Hypnosis, 7*, 8–32.

Erickson, M. H. (1965). The use of symptoms as an integral part of hypnotherapy. *American Journal of Clinical Hypnosis, 8*, 57–65.

Erickson, M. H. (1980). Hypnosis: Its renaissance as a treatment modality. In E. L. Rossi (Ed.), *The collected papers of Milton H. Erickson on hypnosis: Vol. 4. Innovative hypnotherapy* (pp. 52–75). New York: Irvington.

Erickson, M. H., & Rossi, E. L. (1980). Hypnotherapy with a psychotic. In E. L. Rossi, *The collected papers of Milton H. Erickson* (Vol. IV). New York: Irvington.

Erickson, M. H., & Zeig, J. K. (1980). Symptom prescription for expanding the psychotic's world view. In E. L. Rossi (Ed.), *The collected papers of Milton H. Erickson* (Vol. IV). New York: Irvington.

Gilligan, S. (1982). Ericksonian approaches to clinical hypnosis. In J. K. Zeig, *Ericksonian approaches to hypnosis and psychotherapy*. New York: Brunner/Mazel.

Scagnelli-Jobsis, J. (1982). Hypnosis with psychotic patients: A review of the literature and presentation of a theoretical framework. *American Journal of Clinical Hypnosis, 25*, 33–45.

Spiegel, D. (1983). Hypnosis with psychotic patients: Comment on Scagnelli-Jobsis. *American Journal of Clinical Hypnosis, 25*, 289–294.

Zeig, J. K. (1974). Hypnotherapy techniques with psychotic inpatients. *American Journal of Clinical Hypnosis, 17*, 56–59.

Zeig, J. K. (1985). *Ericksonian psychotherapy* (Vol. II). New York: Brunner/Mazel.

Using Subparts in a
Case of Multiple Personality

Claude Millette, M.S.W.

Claude Millette, M.S.W. (Wilfrid Laurier University) is a social worker in Toronto who has experience conducting individual, group and family therapy with substance abusers and mentally retarded adults.

Millette details a utilization approach to a case of multiple personality. Hypnotic and strategic interventions are used to reorganize subparts in the service of the entire personality.

This chapter presents an alternative approach to treating multiple personalities, based on Ericksonian principles. It focuses on the usefulness of hypnotic techniques through visual hallucination, positive reframing, and paradoxical directives. Using visual hallucination of the various personalities, with additional techniques from family therapy, it was possible to increase communication between subpersonalities. It was also possible to reorganize them as subparts in the service of the whole organism and increase their ability as a cohesive group to solve life problems. Positive reframing of the protective function of the dissociation allowed the therapist to maintain rapport with three alter personalities while gradually teaching them alternative behaviors to achieve common goals. Paradoxical directives were used for the containment of self-destructive behaviors within acceptable limits. The above approaches will be illustrated through a case presentation of the successful treatment of a multiple personality.

Multiple personalities are not common occurrences in the practice of most clinicians. Despite an increased interest in this topic in the past few years, most clinicians have not encountered a single case of multiple personality. Consequently these clinicians would be unaware of relevant treatment approaches. This chapter demonstrates how an Ericksonian outlook was useful in planning and implementing therapy of one case involving a multiple personality.

Address reprint requests to Claude Millette, 154 Glenmount Park Road, Toronto, Ontario, Canada M4E 2N4.

To suggest that a single Ericksonian approach exists represents faulty reasoning; one of Erickson's most important contributions has been to convince clinicians that therapy does not have to be a repetitive ritual but can and does necessitate creative thinking by the therapist. This contribution is far reaching and follows an era where the therapist's role was viewed simply as a facilitator. Erickson resurrected the notion of creative thinking as an active process during diagnosis and, most importantly, in the planning and implementation phases of treatment. The case study in this chapter demonstrates that treatment planning based on Ericksonian principles can lead to the development of new techniques.

In this case, the diagnosis of multiple personality was only suspected during the first four sessions. Subsequently, a therapeutic plan was formulated and implemented. The chapter overviews the client-therapist interaction during the first four sessions. The Ericksonian concept of utilization was the central organizing principle behind the approaches used.

Psychosocial Profile

The client, Rosa, was a 32-year-old female health worker of European extraction from an extremely conservative Catholic background who was referred by her employer for the problem of drug abuse. At the time of treatment she was still living at home with an elderly mother who suffered from physical handicaps and hypertension. The client reported losing her father in her mid-teens and having lived away from home for a three-year period to obtain a professional degree. She had spent most of her adult life with her mother. During this period she turned down two marriage proposals, because of her mother's expectations of living with her daughter after the marriage. Both proposals were rejected on the basis of irreconcilable differences between the expectations of her prospective spouse and her mother. Furthermore, during the 10 years of living with her mother she had been subjected to the sexual advances of her mother's boyfriend. This had eventually resulted in sexual assault and an unwanted pregnancy. She had the child but gave it up for adoption.

Rosa appeared to have achieved a certain level of satisfactory adaptation to her life situation up to the age of 26. At this time three events occurred simultaneously which took on crisis proportions. She rejected her second marriage proposal. She was sexually assaulted and became pregnant by her mother's boyfriend. Finally, her mother suffered an accident which incapacitated her physically. Her mother used the physical complaints as a means of demanding more time and attention from her daughter. Subsequent to this, our client found herself in hospital for a wide range of physical ailments. Over the course of the next year she was seen by approximately 15 specialists to assess her various medical concerns. These included diagnosis of multiple sclerosis, colitis, cystitis and asthma. Each of these illnesses seemed to resolve itself and emotional factors were identified as a causal component.

Discovery of a Multiple Personality

In order to understand the development of the case it will be useful to provide a contextual description of the relationship of the therapist and the client prior to the diagnosis of multiple personality. Rosa was seen within the context of behaviorally oriented group therapy in a short-term outpatient program involving daily participation for a three-week period in relaxation-training, assertiveness-training, and problem-solving groups.

Within a few weeks of beginning therapy Rosa reported increasing feelings of depression in the evenings. Group consensus was that she was progressing well in all groups. She felt that she was making positive gains from the therapy. Behavioral analysis of the depression revealed little information other than the onset was consistently at 10:00 p.m. The depression started suddenly with no identifiable trigger or antecedents and would stop almost as suddenly at approximately 1:00 a.m. Rosa was not aware of any negative self-statements during these episodes. She described experiencing a very intense feeling of depression. After the first day the feelings increased in intensity and were accompanied by fantasies of self-mutilation. She also reported having a history of self-harm which she had not previously disclosed. The self-mutilation fantasies were of using razor blades to cut deeply into the upper part of the leg. She became increasingly anxious that the intensity of the fantasies of self-mutilations was increasing to such a degree that she might not be able to resist these thoughts. Her description of her experiences of self-mutilation were consistent with someone in a dissociated state.

The contrast between Rosa's apparent progress in the various treatment groups and the severity and intensity of the depressive episodes, which appeared to be dissociated, led me to consider exploring the depression using a hypnotic approach. Given the short-term duration of the treatment program and the rapidly approaching discharge date (five days), it was felt that a light trance utilizing ideomotor signals might help clarify the situation sufficiently to prepare follow-up plans. Because some unconscious part of the individual is operative in producing a symptom, it is sometimes possible to gain information as the symptom's function by indirect inquiry using ideomotor responses of the subject. Unfortunately, this client seemed to have difficulty using these signals; therefore, a quick shift was made to the use of visual images since she had demonstrated herself in the group therapy sessions to be quite adept at using imagery.

Within this first session Rosa was asked to develop a visualization of a blackboard with images of the words "yes" and "no" appearing in response to the therapist's questions. When she could cooperate I asked the part responsible for the depression to talk. Rosa reported being confused by a strange visual image. She identified a "no" appearing on the board within a square box with a "yes" running around the box. This response was in fact quite confusing to me as well as to Rosa. Further exploration led me to ask whether there was a function to the depression. A second response of similar type was produced with a "yes" inside the box and a "no" floating around the box.

In order to explore the issue of the depressive episodes further Rosa was asked if there were a part of her that felt responsible for the depression. She described obtaining a "yes" that came out clearly toward her and a "no" that faded in the background. At this point I decided the image of the blackboard was not particularly useful in communicating with the parts responsible for some of the difficulties, primarily due to the dissociated character of the responses. Most subjects responding to questioning with ideomotor responses while under trance do so with one response at a time once clearly defined signals for "yes," "no" and "maybe" have been identified. Rosa, however, responded to most questions with a combination of two signals with completely opposite meaning. This produced ambiguous answers to the questions which caused only confusion. This led me to posit the existence of two parts responsible for the contradictions in the message. In order to decrease the ambiguity of the message I decided to increase the complexity of the image.

Rosa was asked if she could create an image representing both the "yes" and the "no" parts. This was framed in vague terms. She questioned whether they should be two images of two women or two men. She was told they could be any image of her choosing. She then identified a man, a woman, and a little girl. The first session involved establishing some kind of signal with this image. Initially contact was made with the little girl and she was asked to raise the right arm for "yes" and the left arm for "no." She was asked, for example, if she would like to grow up. The little girl in the image frowned and Rosa described her as standing with both hands in her pockets, sulking. A treatment contract was considered within the first session. All three parts were asked to consider the possibility of assisting me in helping them, with the understanding that this might require several months of contact. They were given a week to think about this.

It should be noted that the treatment evolved out of the material produced in the first few sessions. The treatment method developed was based partly on the belief that the therapist needs to find a means of communicating with all parts of the individual. After the first session I extensively planned productive ways of using the images. The notion of asking Rosa to describe the ideomotor signals of the three images seemed promising. The primary concern was developing a strategy that would allow the utilization of the elements that developed within the first session. In this sense the use of imagery was based on Rosa's prior success at visualizing for the purpose of imaginal rehearsal of behavioral change.

In the sessions that followed Rosa was asked to sit back and visualize the man, the woman, and the little girl and to report the answers of all three parts. Formal induction was not required as Rosa could readily produce the images simply by closing her eyes. It was possible to ask one question and thereby determine the position of all three parts on the issue. All three parts were instructed to raise the right arm for "yes" and left arm for "no." Verification was made to ensure that all parts understood the task.

This approach differs from the standard ideomotor signalling approach in two respects. First, the ideomotor signals were produced by the parts in the imagery, thereby forcing me to rely on Rosa's observation of the signals. Also, this approach led to the simultaneous production of opposite responses from the various parts. Therefore, I was in a position similar to a family therapist having to monitor and remember the responses of more than one family member. In this way I was able to begin mapping areas of conflict between the various parts and to discover the parts responsible for specific symptoms. It was interesting to notice that the parts could report completely opposite views on a single issue and appeared to have distinct belief systems.

Once I ascertained that it was possible to communicate with all of the parts, the next step was obtaining a treatment contract. Given that Rosa presented personality parts that were powerful enough to produce severe symptoms of depression and self-mutilation it seemed important to attempt to secure their consent before proceeding with treatment. Furthermore, I decided to treat and speak to each part as a distinct individual.

The treatment contract evolved in stages and changed over the period of the first three sessions. At the end of the first session I offered treatment for up to one year on a weekly basis, providing all of the parts agreed. Given that the woman in the imagery had already acknowledged responsibility for the feelings of depression and the fantasies of self-mutilation, she was offered the possibility of showing her agreement by stopping the symptoms for a period of time. She categorically refused to stop the depression but indicated an interest in therapy. Through questioning, it was ascertained that she (the part) felt that Rosa should be punished for Rosa's attitude about her (the part). Her stance was acknowledged as important, although not understood. By the third session a compromise was reached which could be understood as a paradoxical prescription of the symptom. The symptom of the depression was circumscribed to happen at a specific time in the evening and in the setting of her home, with the result that the intensity of the depression was reduced considerably. The goal of this approach was to contain the symptom within manageable limits and to circumscribe it sufficiently that it would not threaten Rosa's life or her ability to work.

In order to achieve this, all of the parts were asked their feelings about Rosa's work. Since all of them felt good about her work, it was easy to use this as leverage with the woman part to limit the depression to the home environment. By the third session some time had been spent exploring the ways in which Rosa communicated with the therapist through the imagery. It was found that the imagery was a useful but time consuming approach which often produced ambiguous information. For example, in response to certain questions that were either ambiguous or unclear one of the images might raise one or both hands up and down in rapid succession, indicating sometimes "yes," sometimes "no." Although it was noted that hesitancy in responding was a good way of determining how committed the images were to their answers the endeavor resembled the game of 20 questions and placed responsibility for information gathering on the therapist.

During the fourth session I obtained an agreement from all of the client's parts to maintain a diary. It was explained that each part could use the diary to communicate either with the therapist or with another part. This diary later became a central source of information regarding issues to be addressed in therapy sessions.

I have emphasized the development of three techniques (which became the foundation of the therapy) and the rationale for their use at the time. This was done to underline the fact that the Ericksonian approach captivates therapists' full attention and forces them to think strategically. In this sense therapists are active in planning and structuring the interaction with clients to achieve maximum understanding of a problem. Therapists are encouraged to utilize everything brought into the treatment context by clients and to devise treatment strategies that take into account clients' needs, personality characteristics and strengths. This includes accepting problems as they are presented by clients. It may also require doing some homework in order to analyze the problem into workable components. Finally, it necessitates a willingness to develop a plan which will restructure the problem components in such a way that the therapist gains therapeutic control of these various components. This aspect of the

Ericksonian approach is often neglected. Therapists are forced to think of a central treatment plan while also keeping alternatives in mind. Treatment planning involves a great deal of work and provides therapists with the internal structure to be spontaneous in the treatment situation itself as it develops. This preliminary work allows therapists a choice of deciding whether or not to follow through with the original plan or consider an alternative. In treatment planning therapists must take into account their own personality characteristics and style of intervention, but most of all, their unique skills. In essence they have to be able to answer the following question for themselves: What can I do with this person?

In this case, the diagnosis of multiple personality was questionable because of the client's reliance on visual information. At that point in time the issue of the diagnosis had not, in fact, been raised. The central concern in this case was finding an approach that would provide maximum contact with parts which appeared dissociated from consciousness and which acknowledged or claimed responsibility for severe symptoms of depression and self-mutilation.

Following the initial contract I conducted an extensive review of the literature on the topic of multiple personalities. Erickson's own work with multiple personalities has been reported in "The Clinical Discovery of a Dual Personality" (1980). In this article he considers significant questions concerning the actual incidence of frequency of multiple personalities, the possibilities for discovery, the clinical nature and character of multiple and secondary personalities, and especially the significant values of this clinical phenomenon as a research problem.

Later developments in the case confirmed that this client presented most of the characteristics attributed to multiple personalities: amnesia, distinct behavioral presentation, many alternating physiological disturbances of the conversion type (Bliss, 1980). The amnesic episodes which were revealed in the treatment involved periods when the client became sexually promiscuous. Finally, she described being completely dissociated during episodes of self-mutilation involving a razor blade. These factors were found to be consistent with the constellation of symptomatology of other cases diagnosed as multiple personality. The literature review revealed that the rationale and purpose of my treatment plan and overall strategy were similar to the approaches of clinicians such as Watkins and Watkins (1980), Beahrs (1982a, 1982b) and Kluft (1984).

In summary, this approach involved the use of visual hallucination of three parts described as a man, a woman, and a child. Communication with the parts of the imagery was achieved through the client's observations of the ideomotor responses produced by each of the various parts and subsequent verbal reports of these to the therapist.

The second approach that proved useful in the first four sessions involved paradoxical prescription of the symptom of depression. With this approach it was possible to maintain contact with the part responsible for this symptom while simultaneously containing the symptom. Having taken the time to get to know the part responsible for the depression, it was possible to find a context for the symptom's occurrence that was acceptable to this part yet not too dangerous for the client. As the interrelationship between parts changed over the course of the next year, this approach was used repeatedly to avert the emergence of new symptoms. For example, paradoxical intervention was used to resolve Rosa's ambivalence about leaving home. Even after reviewing the feeling of the various parts about leaving home, Rosa remained unable to decide to separate from her mother. She was asked to live with her mother for three days. During that period she was to accede to her mother's every wish and desire and to be extra attentive to ensure that her mother could not be critical of anything. Upon her return she reported that she only followed the assignment for a few hours, then spontaneously decided that she could no longer live with her mother. She used the time to secure an apartment. She placed a deposit on an apartment on the first day of her stay with her mother, with a promise to move three weeks later. The next two days were used to find furniture. Following completion of this task, a group discussion with the subparts explored the feelings of all of the parts regarding this issue.

Finally, the third and perhaps most important approach was the use of the diary. In the therapy sessions which followed, the three approaches were linked by a format. Each session started with a review of the client's conscious understanding of the previous week focusing on concrete behavioral goals, tasks and changes such as leaving home, returning to work, her relationship to her mother, her relationship with men. Then the diary material was reviewed, and any discrepancy between the diary material and the client's conscious presentation was noted. The final step involved a return to the use of imagery to explore the dynamics between the parts.

In this process a hierarchy of goals for the session was chosen. For example, should the client consciously verbalize that the week had been uneventful except for a slight disagreement with a male friend, while the diary reported an extreme concern for body image and the use of tension headaches on three occasions to avoid dating, then the issue of this client's relationship to men and difficulties in social intercourse would become a goal for the session.

Often the diary made direct comments about the most important issue for the week. These were then followed up through group discussion with the imagery of the feelings regarding the issue at hand. The following excerpts from the diary will show how issues would be raised for discussion by the parts themselves. In this sense the diary provided the various parts with direct input into the therapy sessions.

Observations by All of the Other Parts about the Little Girl

She just doesn't know how to be good to herself.

Lately, every morning she awakens depleted and frantic over how she's going to summon the energy to get through the day.

Sometimes she takes out her frustrations on objects, and lately she's angry at everything, and constantly fighting all the "other parts."

She's also acting out some long festering resentment over her return to the work world.

Sometimes, in the past the little girl has thought, "I'll get what I want by keeping them thinking I'll be bad. Of course I have to be bad enough to convince them."

Once the goals of the session had been established we returned to the imagery to explore the thoughts and feelings of the various parts related to the problem issue. In this stage the goal of therapy was twofold: The first goal of this stage was to help decrease the amnesic barrier by increasing the amount of information between the parts. In order to do so the parts were treated as a group learning to solve problems. The second goal for this stage was to help the conscious personality or to learn to take an observer's stance between the parts and act as a mediator in the problem-solving attempts.

Excerpts from the diary best demonstrate the underlying personalities of the various parts as they presented themselves. Diary excerpts from the first few sessions will be contrasted with those from later sessions. These will give body to the notion of conducting group therapy for the various parts of multiple personalities. The early excerpts symbolize subpersonalities that are very rigid in the content of their productions and also in the style or pattern of their interaction. The first two excerpts present the personality of the man in the imagery.

The Man in Imagery (the Distinguished Thinker) Speaks

The older I grow, the more clearly I perceive the dignity and winning beauty of simplicity in thought, conduct, and speech; a desire to simplify all that is complicated and to treat everything with the greatest naturalness and clarity. Successful living is an endless quest for the simple, the clear, the true. It is a journey toward simplicity and a triumph over confusion. All the truly deep people have at the core of their being the genius to be simple or to know how to seek simplicity.

Rosa, you have been feeling somewhat angry that more people haven't come to your aid. The problem may be that you haven't allowed others to become aware of your distress. Your pain cannot be understood or shared by anyone unless you allow it to be known. By *gradually* letting down the walls that hide your struggle you can give selected *people* a chance to respond empathetically to you. Try not to give up on the whole human race if the feelings that you share are misunderstood by someone.

In both these excerpts the man appears to be the stereotype of the wise old man. The title "the distinguished thinker" was chosen by the man himself. It is appropriate as it symbolically summarizes the man's function. "He" appeared to be constantly providing the "little girl" with advice. The two excerpts are also fairly typical of the early stages in that the advice given was framed in vague and often ambiguous generalizations. The advice was often presented as statements of truths which had universal validity.

The "man" conceptualized his role as the protector of the "little girl" and prided himself on being more aware of the little girl's feelings than she was herself. Although he did not appear to have the ability to put his thoughts into action he was able to explore feelings from a rational perspective. Unfortunately, he sometimes erred in the direction of overintellectualizing an issue to the extent that it lost its impact. While he sometimes appeared wise in his advice, he could also be rigidly moralistic.

The next excerpt demonstrates the personality of the "woman" as she presented herself.

Messages from the Woman in Imagery

I know how right I am.

If you loved me, you wouldn't be acting this way.

I don't love you the way you are.

You never listen.

You always do this to me.

You know how much I count on you.

I'm very disappointed in you.

This shows you don't really care.

If you loved me, you'd…

After all I've done for you, this is the thanks I get.

You are denying what you feel.

I'm right, you're wrong.

I feel jealous.

I don't want to discuss it.

It's all your fault.

Touching isn't allowed and hugging is absolutely forbidden.

Do what you want, but don't come crying to me.

You're ashamed of me.

I'll keep up the pressure only as long as I sense any uncertainty.

As can be noted, the style of presentation of the thoughts is quite different. The "woman" was not verbose. In fact, she required much support to express herself verbally. She perceived punishment through physiological symptomatology and acting out as more powerful means of getting her wishes. She acknowledged responsibility for many of the symptoms and appeared to be in a constant battle with the "little girl" to have her needs met.

In a different way the woman was very rigid and unable to compromise. It was only after a few months that the woman started to acknowledge that group problem solving was more productive for her than the previous method of acting out. Over time, the emphasis was placed on increasing the amount of information flowing from one part to the other by helping them learn to talk to each other in the imagery sessions.

Another aspect of this woman part was that she was actively involved in sexual acting out, which involved taking control of the client's body. She reported going to drinking establishments and behaving in ways which appeared totally out of character to the central personality. She also reported occasionally seducing men without understanding how or why she did so and described an instance of inviting an elderly cab driver to her room to pay for the fare.

In the early stages the "little girl" was never present in the diary except as a recipient of advice from both the man and the woman. From these it was possible to realize that a strong alliance existed between the man and the little girl at the expense of the woman. This alliance allowed both the man and the little girl to keep the woman under their control most of the time.

The following diary excerpts will demonstrate a change in the interaction between the parts that was more typical of the later sessions.

Dialogue between the Parts in the Imagery

Dialogue 1

Little Girl:	How can I do what I'm scared of doing?
Man:	I'll help you be scared.
Girl:	I don't want help. And I don't think you help a person by making her scared.
Man:	You're more than scared — you're frightened of feeling scared. I guess it's frightening for you to feel. It's safer for you to be numb, separate, and lonely.
Girl:	Her face went blank.
Man:	You see what you've just done to feel safe from me?
Girl:	Leave me alone, I want to be mad at you.
Man:	No, I won't leave you alone, and I won't let you get mad at me.
Girl:	How can you stop me?
Man:	I already have.
Girl:	It doesn't sound like such a good idea, you know.
Man:	If you don't trust anyone, that includes yourself. I can get scared, knowing that unless my life and safety are in danger, it's only a matter of time... and what I do... until the fear subsides. If I can't help myself, I can at least turn to others for help.
Girl:	So I don't trust anyone else, but I trust myself.
Man:	If you trusted yourself, you could be flexible and if we don't have to change "self-destructive" or wasteful patterns,* we won't. But, basically we are resourceful creatures and, if we can tolerate deprivation and fear,

---

*"Little girl" does these self-destructive things because they make her feel in control and safe

we can also change and learn how to have more healthy behavior and different values.

Girl: But it's all I've got.

Man: Then let's find you more.

Girl: How do I know that if I give this up I'll have more?

Man: If you don't give it up, you can't ever have more.

Girl: So there's no guarantee?

Man: You will discover your own strengths and resources if you are deprived of your self-harm (etc.) for security.

Girl: You want me to give up my only security?

Man: So that you can have more from other sources.

Girl: Why can't I get these other sources of security first?

Man: Can you talk a junkie out of heroin while he's stoned?

Girl: That's easy for you to say. You don't have to change anything.

Man: Everything that happens between us is easier for me than for you. I'm always aware of that. It doesn't mean that we can excuse you from the...won't be noticed, or not appreciated, or not supported.

Girl: So you're going to help me struggle and be scared. Big deal, I think that's the worst offer anybody ever made me. (*But she managed a smile.*)

Dialogue 2

Little Girl: How come I feel so young here?

Woman: I think all of us feel a little younger when people take care of us. Maybe you've been trying to be too old— pushing yourself too far.

Girl: Maybe.

Woman: Maybe you could stop trying so hard. You always push so hard in so many directions that I worry you might burn yourself out one way or another.

Girl: I'm always afraid. Sometimes I don't know what I'm afraid of, but when I do, it's a fear of falling behind, of everybody getting ahead of me. I just feel like if I'm not careful I'll become nothing. Invisible.

Woman: (*Smiled at her with real affection*) I guess you want to be shiny, huh?

Girl: Nodded.

Woman: If that's what you want, I wonder who you want to share it with.

Girl: What do you mean?

Woman: You sound so lonely. You're full of "what's" but no "who." It seems like there's no one in your life, no one that you feel touched by.

These last excerpts were entitled Dialogues 1 and 2 by the client. These dialogues became the point of departure for group sessions in the imagery. Many of the themes in these dialogues resurfaced as the therapy progressed. It can be seen that in these dialogues a problem-solving process has been activated. Characteristics of the various subpersonalities are unclear at any point in the process. This was resolved by asking each part to assess and summarize changes that they had made over time. The next diary excerpt demonstrates this last point rather clearly.

Messages from the Little Girl to the Other Parts

I still appreciate that the other parts talk and tell me things. I don't feel like I'm in the room alone. If I were, I'd get confused and wander. Whether I'll try the things you told me I don't know. I know they'll depress me because they are happening in *my* life, with me privately. That's the reason abandonment scares me so much. I'm afraid of being abandoned by other people, since I long ago abandoned myself. So there's no *one* there when I'm alone. I am so camouflaged by my experiences and you are asking me to accept some part of myself (nervousness, for example) and go on from there.

I always like it when you give me directives. I become much more aware of my behavior, not as something magical, but just as behavior. Last night I became aware of how the *fear* starts. I think of something, I hold my breath to listen, that hurts my stomach, makes me feel like I'm in an elevator and can't get off. And before I know it, I'm on an unlucky floor. Your methods are comforting. You still seem to think that you can ask me questions that I will answer helpfully or with insight. You treat me with interest.

In this last excerpt the "little girl" is able to communicate her reaction to the other parts. She also demonstrates that she had begun to deal with some of her feelings using feedback from the other parts. More than with any other form of pathology, multiple personalities provide a special challenge to a therapist in that many of the subpersonalities of the client possess more knowledge regarding a client than the therapist does. This approach requires the ability to deal with the multiple personality as a group of personalities which need to learn to coordinate their efforts. In this sense therapists need to be able to recognize the unique needs of each personality and to help each learn to use the group of personalities as a whole to solve problems. This implies that therapists do not allow themselves to join any of the parts in an alliance against the others. This is a distinct departure from the traditional approach to multiple personalities.

The central features of the traditional approaches to the treatment of multiple personalities were originally identified by Brandsma and Ludwig; in 1974 they identified five treatment options for multiple personalities. Greaves (1980) proposes that three of these five options correspond to the treatments most often offered: forced fusion; support resurgence of the main personality; and focus on the healthiest personality. Other clinicians (e.g., Allison, 1974; Beahrs, 1982; Kluft, 1984; Watkins & Watkins, 1980) are in the process of developing alternative approaches which involve considering the multiple parts of the individual and working progressively toward the integration of these parts. The central features common to all of these approaches are a respect for the multiplicity within the individual and the willingness to accept the parts as allies in the treatment process. These are in keeping with the general principles outlined in this article.

One difficulty in dealing with multiple personalities is the series of crises which occur. In this case paradoxical prescriptions served to contain symptoms in crisis periods in order to avert hospitalization. The approach outlined in this chapter involves the use of three specific techniques designed to meet the needs and characteristics of a specific client and allow the therapist to have a therapeutic input: the use of visual hallucination of subpersonalities for problem solving, paradoxical prescriptions for symptom containment, and finally, use of a diary. This case demonstrates a change in the relationships between parts presented by an unusual client.

Little attention has been paid here to any theory of multiple personality because a single case presentation usually cannot be extrapolated to other cases. It should be mentioned, nevertheless, that the approaches used in this analysis are consistent with the formulation of Beahrs (1982a, 1982b) on multiple personalities. The overall strategy of reducing amnesic barriers is consistent with Erickson's approach to multiple personalities. On the one hand communication with subparts demonstrates respect for all aspects of the individual and willingness to rely on information from the unconscious. The second aspect which is important involves willingness to devise a specific strategy based on the information received in the therapeutic encounter. This strategy was based not on therapeutic theory but on utilizing the client's characteristics for her own benefits.

Successful treatment for this woman was eventually achieved by developing her ability to consider other parts of herself and use them in the process of solving problems. Drastic changes occurred in her life: She was able to move out of her mother's house and live on her own for a period of two years for the first time in her life. Ten months after therapy had been terminated she wrote, "In looking over the notes, I found myself recalling many memories, yet at times I'd come across something that at this point I don't remember writing. It has helped me discover a self I didn't know lay within me and it has certainly been an adventure into unexplored and undiscovered parts...I no longer feel alone."

In conclusion, Ericksonian principles provide a solid epistemological formulation for treatment planning and treatment implementation for a case of multiple personality. The principles can be summarized as respect and acceptance of all parts of the individual, utilization of client characteristics, and willingness to accept parts of the individual as cotherapists. One of the drawbacks of this approach is that it can lead the novice therapist to feelings of insecurity since it does not provide a complete prepackaged outline of procedures to be followed. Instead, the development of the approach is based on the clinician's careful assessment of each client's situation and the clinician's ability to plan a treatment strategy according to those characteristics. Thus, after careful analysis of the situation, the approach to clients should be different in each case and determined, in part, by taking into consideration both client and therapist characteristics.

References

Allison, R. B. (1974). A new treatment approach for multiple personalities. *American Journal of Clinical Hypnosis, 17*, 15–32.

Beahrs, J. O. (1982a). *Unity and multiplicity. Multilevel consciousness of self in hypnosis, psychiatric disorder and mental health.* New York: Brunner/Mazel.

Beahrs, J. O. (1982b). Co-consciousness: A common denominator. *American Journal of Clinical Hypnosis, 26*, 100–113.

Bliss, E. L. (1980). Multiple personalities: A report on 14 cases with implications for schizophrenia and hysteria. *Archives of General Psychiatry, 37*, 1388–1396.

Erickson, M. H. (1980). The clinical discovery of a dual personality. In E. L. Rossi (Ed.), *The collected papers of Milton H. Erickson on hypnosis, Vol. III, Hypnotic investigation of psychodynamic processes* (pp. 264–567). New York: Irvington.

Greaves, G. B. Multiple personalities, 165 years after Mary Reynolds. *The Journal of Nervous and Mental Disease, 168* (10), 577–596.

Kluft, R. (1984). Treatment of multiple personality disorder. *Psychiatric Clinics of North America, 7*(1), 9–31.

Watkins, J. G., & Watkins, H. W. (1980). Ego states and hidden observers. *Journal of Altered States of Consciousness, 5*(1), 3–18.

Cross-Cultural Ericksonian Techniques with Mexican American Clients

G. Dean Bathel, A.C.S.W., and
Carlos R. Carreon, A.C.S.W.

G. Dean Bathel, M.S.W. (Arizona State University), A.C.S.W., is presently Clinical Supervisor of O'Rielly Care Center and in private practice in Tucson, Arizona. Carlos Ronaldo Carreon, M.S.W. (Arizona State University), A.C.S.W., is Regional Clinical Supervisor of Human Affairs International and in private practice in Tucson, Arizona.

Ericksonian utilization techniques can effect change in Mexican American clients. These techniques provide a powerful combination for change when used with strategies that tap the closely intertwined systems of blood family and extended nonblood family.

Milton Erickson's greatest contribution is the concept of utilization. His most enduring legacy will not be specific trance techniques or any particular change strategy; it will be his way of thinking about people. For Erickson, differences between people were opportunities. Keeping this orientation in mind, we will examine therapy with Mexican Americans. What is their experience? What do they, in varying degrees, bring to therapy? How can it be utilized?

A significant aspect of the Mexican American experience is particular relationship structures that have been developed and reinforced during thousands of years of Mexican American history. Especially significant is the *compradazgo-amistad* system (extended nonblood family). We have found that it is possible for sensitive therapists to enter this system. Once entered, acceptance can replace resistance; intimacy can replace caution; confidence can replace doubt. For this to occur, in many instances it is not necessary for the client and the therapist to be of the same color.

Address reprint requests to G. Dean Bathel, O'Rielly Care Center, St. Joseph's Hospital, Tucson, AZ 85732, or Carlos Carreon, 102 W. Ohio, Tucson, AZ 85703.

Historical Influences

The term Mexican American is used here to describe the mestizo, Spanish-speaking people of the Southwest United States. This term denotes the mixture between Mexican and Anglo American cultures. It adds the voice of Anglo American culture to form a trio of influences continually in flux, i.e., Indian, Spanish, and Anglo American.

Mexicano, Spanish American, and Mexican American are cultural labels that reflect varied historical influences. Mexicano is the self-label most frequently used by Mexican Americans among themselves. It is derived from the Aztec peoples who ruled Mexico at the time of the Spanish conquest. It reflects the heritage bequeathed to the descendants of the large, well-ordered Indian cities that dotted the landscape of pre-Columbian Mexico. Many traditions, works, beliefs, and customs are traceable primarily to Aztec and other Nahua-speaking people in the area (Friedlander, 1975).

Aspects of current Mexican American nonblood family relationships echo the distant Aztec past. Warrior brotherhoods within each ancient city were the primary military, social and religious structures that defined behavior. They served to augment and enrich the principle of family to the extent that any individual, by virtue of membership in the brotherhood, was as close as a biological family member. Brotherhoods became parallel families and were extended to include women and children. There was no such thing as an identity distinct from the brotherhood (Diaz-Guerrero, 1982). This brotherhood, or extended nonblood family, has survived centuries of onslaught from religion, immigration, war, and acculturation attempts of many kinds. But various conflicts have been acquired which shape the Mexican American's experience.

It is important to note that 80% of Mexican Americans live in close proximity to their *compadres* and *comadres* (nonblood brothers and sisters) (Keefe et al., 1978). As a result, Anglo practitioners may see Mexican Americans in conflict over the following assimilation issues: interdependence versus independence; hierarchy versus equality; field dependence versus field independence; relationship identity versus individual identity; present orientation versus future orientation; family values versus career values; social interaction versus social isolation.

Clinical Application

Because most Mexican Americans handle emotional and behavioral difficulties within both their family systems (blood and nonblood) and their religious systems, when they come to therapy those systems have probably proved unequal to the task. Therefore, Mexican Americans often approach therapy with a great deal of anxiety, shame, and desperation. This offers the therapist an opportunity to fill a family role.

The following steps are instrumental. First, take a thorough history. Particular attention should be paid to these details: the level of acculturation; the orientation to family commitment; the level of communalism; the family role the client holds; the integration of others as it affects self-identity; the balance of thought and feeling; the significance of spiritual power; and the impact of family and religious rituals. Second, assume a respectful attitude, acknowledging by nonverbal cues that it is a privilege to be speaking about clients' personal lives and the family history. Third, elicit as completely as possible visual, auditory, and kinesthetic representations of the client's relationship model or models. It is also not necessary for the client to be actually living within these models. They can be idealized relationships. What is essential is that the client has a cognitive and emotional niche for a *compadre* (nonblood brothers and sisters) or perhaps an *hermano de fe* (brother of belief).

It may be comforting for the non-Mexican American therapist to note, it has been our experience that the criteria for accepting another individual in *la familia* is primarily kinesthetic, not visual. It appears to be more important for the client to *feel* that the therapist is not unlike a family member, rather than that he or she look like one.

Confident that being a *gringo* is not a stop sign, the therapist can proceed to the fourth step, sharing isomorphic metaphors, stories, and experiences concerning healing relationships. We have found this fourth step to be essential. Caution, however, is advised. For example, we once worked with an elementary teacher who had good rapport with his Mexican American students until he disclosed that he hated his brother and had not seem him in years. The Mexican American students thought he was "nuts." How could they trust anyone who openly talked that way about his brother? Unfortunately, the teacher was unaware of the value placed on family relationships.

In the early stages of the therapy, important family information is elicited, reinforced, and paced in a manner that is comfortable, natural, and reassuring to the client. As the client relaxes into a more familial role, the therapist can begin to lead the client unconsciously to accept the therapist into his idea of *la familia*. By respectfully behaving in the "as if frame" modeled on the real or idealized structure provided by the client, the therapist can start to elicit the emotional correlates of a powerful nonblood family ally.

Many therapists may find that this approach runs counter to their therapeutic training. Assuming the professional role implies therapeutic distance. Positioning oneself in this manner is contraindicated with many Mexican Americans. Consider the following:

> The Anglo-dominated medical system has developed a device for protecting modesty that works well for certain patients, especially Anglos. It is called "assuming the professional role." Even if patients are close personal friends of the health professionals, the physicians or nurses (or whomever) take on impersonal roles as "healers" rather than "friends" during healing interactions, and this sets up social distance between the professionals and their patients.... If, instead, the healers assumed a close personal role and symbolically moved closer to their patients, the perceived intimacy of the situation would become too pronounced and the patients would have to remove themselves from the interaction....
>
> The case appears to be reversed for many Mexican American patients. For them, the assumptions of impersonal professional roles by healers act as barriers to patient-healer interactions. When doctors take on this role, they are perceived as being cold and aloof, and much too difficult to talk to about intimate subjects. Instead, the patients' expectations are that healers should symbolically move closer, rather than backing away. When physicians reduce the social distance between themselves and their patients, they temporarily become as though they were "one of the family," and therefore intimacy is acceptable.... Therefore, when healers establish a highly personalized interaction with Mexican American patients, they are able to protect modesty by drawing close, becoming "one of the family," and therefore becoming an acceptable repository for intimate information about their patients that cannot be shared with "nonfamily" in the outside world. (Trotter, 1982, pp. 324–325)

Also, do not be reticent to express overt compassion. For example, during the course of therapy the Anglo author (Bathel) shed tears in front of his Mexican American client. Unexpectedly, he was henceforth regarded as family, as was noted by verbal and nonverbal cues. In effect, a display of compassion elicited the whole structure, i.e., family membership. In addition, the client did not appear to need reaffirmation of the therapist's overt compassion during the remaining sessions.

Two points should be made here. The therapist in the case example is a moderate fellow. Once in the family system, he did not test the new relationship by trying to elicit totally foreign behaviors from the client. Also, the authors are not advocating "tear therapy." What we are saying is that genuine, overt compassion has its place in therapy. Mexican Americans come to therapy to be healed. Healing for them is most often heart to heart, not head to head.

It is at this point that trance can be most effective. It is helpful to use induction language that is linked to significant memories, experiential learnings, and natural trance states within the culture. Given the material discussed so far, religious and family rituals and ceremonies can themselves be utilized as avenues to trance states. These are not the only natural resources available. The possibilities are limited only by experience and imagination.

We also employ Erickson, Rossi and Rossi's (1976) five-step paradigm of sequential induction and suggestion: 1) inward focusing; 2) defusing habitual mind sets; 3) activating unconscious searches; 4) activating personal associations and lines of thought; and 5) recognizing hypnotic responses. Their design is elegant and practical:

Religious and family trance states powerfully focus the client's attention on vivid internal memories that contain rich metaphorical material (step 1). For example, most Mexican Americans are Catholics. Whether practicing or not, they have probably had the experience of the Mass. It is our belief that trance occurs many times during Mass. One of the basic tenets of the Church is that the world is not as it appears. It is full of patron saints, angels, and intercessors. The Virgin de Guadalupe, a patron saint of the Mexican American people, is thought to create miracles, visions, and intercede on behalf of families. Anyone who has ever prayed the rosary or heard a Novina in Spanish is well aware of trance. This rich, full world of experience can frame trance as a sanctified healing phenomenon.

The metaphoric implications for Ericksonian therapy are rich. Resurrection, renewal, sacrifice, change, metamorphosis, and emergence are all religious and cultural themes available to the therapist. Candles and incense burn and are transformed. The lines between psychotherapy and religion become blurred. We are not advocating that therapists rush to take vows of chastity and poverty or take Holy Orders, but rather that they learn to utilize the opportunity for trance states based upon religious experience.

Another natural context in which trance occurs that can assist inward focusing is family rituals, stories or legends. The rhythmic clapping of hands making tortillas, the songs of Alabados (songs of praise), everyone's *tata* (grandfather) rode with Pancho Villa or saw the *Cabillo Blanco* of Emiliano Zapata (an historic folk hero who never died but will return on his white horse), and stories of a Mexico long lost in the memories of their grandfathers, all provide rich material that access trance states. Specific experiences may vary, but broad references are available. Trance states sanctioned by the church and through cultural legends and warmed by the family can create intense rapport.

After combining religious and family memories and metaphors, suggestions can be made to link the therapist to the *compradazgo-amistad* system, i.e., "What you are experiencing is not unlike experiences you have had with your *comadre*." The client can become mildly confused (step 2) and initiate an unconscious search to make sense of these suggestions (step 3). Remember that prior to trance a great deal of therapeutic activity has been focused on special nonblood family relationships. Capitalizing on the work and information gathered during the initial sessions, the therapist continues to assist the client to mobilize personal family associations and sequences (step 4). As Erickson and Rossi (1979) point out:

> Suggestions made during trance frequently function like keys turning the tumblers of a patient's associative processes within the locks of certain mental frameworks that have already been established. A number of workers (Weitzenhoffer, 1957; Schneck, 1970, 1975) have described how what is said before trance is formally induced can enhance hypnotic suggestion. We agree and emphasize that effective trance work is usually preceded by a preparatory phase during which we help patients create an optimal attitude and belief system for therapeutic responses. (p. 2)

It is during steps 2 through 4 that some of the boundaries between therapist and family can disappear. Other than classic physiological phenomenon during trance, one can ratify that trance has been successful by watching and listening to how the client responds to the therapist after trance (step 5). Such words as *hermano* (brother) or *hermana* (sister) will start to be applied to the therapist, often outside of the client's awareness. Feedback also comes in the form of increased self-disclosure, touching, and positive affect.

Relationships transform both the client and therapist. For some therapists the experience of having a Mexican American family relationship, if only for an hour a week, can be uncomfortable. The nature of these techniques may lead therapists to evaluate their own family experience, religious flexibility, and relationship styles.

Also be aware that when entering the family system, the therapist is embued with power and hierarchical standing. Intimacy in this system does not imply equality. In American culture, the political ideology of democracy has sometimes been translated into the relationship principle of equality. Mexican Americans are not deluded by this myth. For Mexican Americans there are no relationships without hierarchy. Therefore, a statement by a therapist such as, "You and I are equal," has no referent. Also note that between *family* members, compliance is more important than individual freedom. For example, we have found that many will carry out tasks because they thought they were told to, not because they agreed to. For some Anglo Americans, being right is more important than being happy. For most Mexican Americans, being right at the expense of relationship is a peculiarly foreign phenomenon.

Case Illustration

Ruben was a 30-year-old Mexican American man who lived in Tucson all of his life. A resident of the city's "barrio," Ruben maintained many Mexican customs, but more importantly Ruben lived in a world view and a value system based upon the Mexican past. Well aware of the history of racism in the Southwest, Ruben came into treatment suspicious of Anglo institutions and cautious of Anglos in general. He grew up in a bilingual household and spoke English fluently and Spanish expressively. Catholic by upbringing, the church continued to shape Ruben's world view without regard to his attendance at Mass.

Ruben's marriage of eleven years was in grave trouble. He and his wife had been drifting apart for some time. He failed to recognize the early signs of a relationship becoming tired and ritualized. He relied on the external factors of an eleven-year marriage and the couple's two children to bind them together, even though the marriage was decaying internally. He sought advice and help from his parents and was told that since he was the man of the house it was his responsibility to keep the family together. How was unclear. His *compadres* were an integral part of his and his wife's life. They helped marry them and were the godparents of their children. They were supportive in every possible way except helping him decide what to do. They didn't know how to make things different, but knew he should do everything he could for the sake of the children.

Ruben felt ineffective and hopeless, despondent, depressed, humiliated and confused. He decided to seek therapy. He had some idea of what therapy was about and sought to connect with a therapist only as a last resort.

The first meeting was anticipated with great trepidation. Ruben reported feeling that he hated going into treatment. The therapist was Anglo—obviously Anglo. Ruben was offered coffee and ushered into a pleasant office with pictures of the therapist's family outings on the walls. The therapist took a relaxed pose, stretched out his legs and engaged in pleasant conversation with Ruben. The therapist asked about Ruben's family and then shared some information about his own brothers, sisters, and friends.

As Ruben talked he began to feel more comfortable and felt a personal connection with the therapist that was somehow familiar and yet surprising. Ruben liked the fact that the therapist was respectful by letting him get to the point of the visit in his own time and in his own way. With considerable shame Ruben recounted his situation, confusion and depression. The therapist mirrored Ruben's downward gaze, soft voice, and slow speech. The therapist told stories about other men who had come to see him to let Ruben know he understood. Ruben agreed to come back. Several sessions proceeded in a similar fashion.

During these sessions, the therapist continued to gather information from the client's representation of his problems and his personal manifestation of the *compradazgo-amistad* system. Stories were used as metaphors with anecdotes to match Ruben's experience, and this led him to a stronger relationship with the therapist. In addition, concrete tasks were given to increase the client's activity level. Interspersed throughout the sessions, the therapist slowly took more and more liberties that characterized the model of intimacies that the client had shared with his own *compadres*. The therapist carefully observed the client's speech, behavior and affect to note any discomfort, as increasing self-disclosure was suggested. The subject of trance was slowly introduced and connected to their previous work. At the beginning of the sixth session, the therapist moved into a new phase.

The therapist began to talk to Ruben about what it felt like to have brothers and *compadres* to talk with. Ruben explained how it felt and heard how the therapist had similar relationships. Ruben was then asked to think back (step 1) and remember how it felt to be talking to one of his brothers or *compadres*. How did the comfort, acceptance and warmth affect the chest, the body temperature, the smile on his face. The therapist then said, "You can have a similar relationship with me. Why not settle back and enjoy the possibilities of having a different *compadre*, if only for an hour?" (step 2). After some initial confusion during step 2, Ruben seemed to begin an internal search to make sense of his feelings regarding an Anglo *compadre* (step 3). The therapist moved physically closer and said, "Things can feel the same. You can settle back and enjoy the way your eyes close, breathing changes, etc." (step 4). Ruben closed his eyes and drifted into a comfortable trance. Trance affirmations followed (step 5).

Basic Principles

For those who are not familiar with Mexican American culture, much of the above information may be new. The following concrete steps are offered as a guide for working with Mexican American clients in a culturally sensitive, Ericksonian framework:

1) Know the general cultural patterns that are present in your region. This may involve exploration of the history of the area and how it affects

the present. Accept the existence of cultural differences. Also know that there are more similarities than differences between or among cultures. In order to hear and feel rituals that reflect inner realities, attendance at fiestas or religious services may be helpful. A Mexican American mentor can be very helpful; such a cultural guide can explain the meanings and functions of customs. Compare your own customs, family experiences, and religious rituals to those found in the Mexican American community. This may render some interesting insights into fascinating differences and useful similarities.

2) After developing a general feel for Mexican American patterns, explore with the client how they individually manifest their culture. Personal history, level of acculturation, and familiarity with traditional structures are all useful guideposts.

3) Listen to the experiences the client has had with Anglos in the past. Build upon the strengths of that history. Acknowledge negative experiences, and gracefully separate yourself from them if you are Anglo.

4) Start consciously to access the *compradazgo-amistad* system by respectfully pacing both the existing and idealized structures.

5) If the *compradazgo-amistad* system has not fully emerged, use trance to potentiate the response using the five-step paradigm previously discussed.

6) Finally, use the diagnostic and historical information to design therapy which retrieves the necessary life experiences and suitably reorganizes them.

Therapists can utilize historically based relationship structures and trance experiences to build intense rapport. Azteca-Mexican, Spanish and Anglo cultures have all contributed to the mosaic of Mexican American culture. Cross-cultural treatment is enhanced through the use of not only Ericksonian trance techniques, but more importantly through the use of the Ericksonian principle of utilization that was based on Erickson's inquisitive way of thinking about people and cultures.

References

Diaz-Guerrero, D. D. (1982). *Psychologia del Mexicano*. Mexico D.F.: Editorial Trillas S.A. de C.V.

Erickson, M. A., & Rossi, E. L. (1979). *Hypnotherapy: An exploratory casebook*. New York: Irvington.

Erickson, M., Rossi, E., & Rossi, S. (1976). *Hypnotic realities*. New York: Irvington.

Friedlander, J. (1975). *Being Indian in Hueyapon: A study of forced identity in contemporary Mexico*. New York: St. Martin.

Keefe, S. E., Padilla, A. M., & Carlos, M. G. (1978). *Emotional support system in two cultures: a comparison of Mexican American and Anglo American*. University of California, Spanish Speaking Mental Health Center, 1978.

Schneck, J. (1970). Prehypnotic suggestions. *Perceptual and Motor Skills, 30,* 826.

Schneck, J. (1975). Prehypnotic suggestion in psychotherapy. *American Journal of Clinical Hypnosis, 17,* 158–159.

Trotter, R. (1982). Contrasting model of healer's role: South Texas case examples. *Hispanic Journal of Behavioral Sciences, 4*(3).

Weitzenhoffer, A. (1957). *General techniques of hypnotism.* New York: Grune & Stratton.

Transcultural Issues in Ericksonian Hypnotherapy

Madeleine M. Richeport, Ph.D.

Madeleine M. Richeport, Ph.D. (New York University) is affiliated with the office of Transcultural Education and Research, Department of Psychiatry, University of Miami School of Medicine. Anthropological investigations of spiritism and cultural trance are a major focus of her research and endeavors.

Richeport surveys the importance of anthropological understanding in Erickson's approach. In order to tailor treatment, it is important for a therapist to take into consideration cultural learnings. Guidelines are presented for culturally appropriate hypnotherapy. From an anthropological perspective, Erickson is described as a shamanistic healer.

Erickson (1966) once commented that doctors from around the world would question him as to "'What is meant by a resistant patient?' They explain in their countries the prestige of a professional man is sufficient to effect both ready trance inductions and remarkably effective immediate responses to hypnotic suggestion. One should keep in mind the fact that cultural factors are often highly significant variables in the use of hypnosis in the healing arts" (p. 173). This chapter deals with the factors that affect the delivery of culturally appropriate hypnotherapy. In examining Erickson's work, one of the ways he accomplished this was to utilize a transcultural perspective.

The Transcultural Approach

A transcultural approach allows for a synthesis between anthropological and psychiatric theory and practice. It takes into account not only the

The author gratefully acknowledges the valuable suggestions on this chapter of Elizabeth M. Erickson, Hilton M. Lopez, Harriet P. Lefley, and Hazel H. Weidman, and the assistance of Carmen Rivera.

Madeleine M. Richeport, Ph.D., is affiliated with the Office of Transcultural Education and Research, Department of Psychiatry, University of Miami School of Medicine, and is Consultant to the Secretariat of Mental Health, Commonwealth of Puerto Rico. Address correspondence to Box 7556, Santurce, PR 00916.

orthodox biomedical system of knowledge and practices, but also the patient's system. On a personal level, a transcultural approach becomes a transpersonal one, which takes both patient and therapist symbols and meanings into consideration (Weidman, 1983). Erickson often said, "When you listen to patients, you want to be sure that you see things from their point of view" (Erickson, 1979). In the Department of Psychiatry at the University of Miami, with which I am affiliated, this approach was pioneered by anthropologist Hazel H. Weidman and psychiatrist James N. Sussex. Programs in Miami have demonstrated that culturally sensitive health care is necessary to serve the many ethnic groups in the city (Weidman, 1978, 1979).

One case example described by Weidman (1985) will illustrate the necessity of this approach. A black nurse called Weidman with great trepidation in her voice, reporting that she had a patient in the Emergency Room who was cursed by Jamaica Joe (a local root doctor), and who said he would die at 12:00 noon. It was 10:00 a.m. at the time. A call was made to a Guyanese faculty member who trained in psychiatry in Jamaica. He told the patient, "I know what your problem is." He took him into his office where he performed some ritual acts and applied substances to get him through 12:00. Following a two-hour recovery, the patient felt well enough to go home. In a follow-up interview, the patient said that he felt fine and that everything was taken care of. Health professionals might have said that this was nonsensical superstition and taken their chances with a psychodynamic approach, which would have been inappropriate and culturally insensitive. It is possible that the patient might have dropped dead from psychogenic causes right in front of them (see Lex, 1974). This is a dramatic example, but evaluation research of the Miami programs, which provide culturally appropriate care from professionals trained in a transcultural approach, demonstrated that they were more efficacious than orthodox mental health programs in reducing dropout rates, hospitalizations, and recidivism (Lefley, 1984; Lefley & Bestman, 1984; Lefley & Pedersen, 1986).

Unlike many therapists who worry about using strategies which seem to foster delusional systems, Erickson was ready to utilize the patients' beliefs (even if they opposed his own) if he felt that by doing so, the patient would be able to function more adequately. Erickson described a case in which he utilized belief in spirits:

One case example concerns an Indian couple, man and wife, became obsessed with the idea they could tip tables. In the hospital they demonstrated it to me. They could tip tables and bad spirits would take over; they assured me that a bad spirit followed them around and took control of them. So I helped them tip a table. I know more about tipping a table than they did... Pretty soon the table-tipping disclosed that there was a weak good spirit there *also*, and another weak good spirit and I started adding all the weak good spirits. Their total strength exceeded the strength of the evil spirit. (cited in Richeport, 1985a, p. 546)

Where change is impossible, Erickson channeled the problem behavior into a socially acceptable area. Just as the Guyanese doctor did not try to convince the patient that he was not hexed, Erickson did not try to change the beliefs in spirits, only their meaning from evil to good.

Another example of Erickson's appreciation of factors other than biomedical is his consideration of cross-cultural, historical, and individual variations. He could never accept that one therapy worked for everyone.

Freud devised psychoanalysis to fit all peoples, of all ages, of both sexes, in all situations, in all cultures, in all times. When I was an infant there were two ways of traveling, by horse or by train. Along came buses and cars and altered that. Then came the propeller plane and altered that. With the jet plane, sailing became obsolete. I've discovered in the last few years that it's easier to get a complicated machine repaired on Mars than to get your car fixed down the block. There have been a lot of changes. In therapy you should have a perspective. Freud was European and what was the perspective in Europe in Freud's day? (Erickson, 1979)

Erickson was fascinated by the way communication is patterned differently in different cultures. In this area, he admired the work of Ray L. Birdwhistle (1970), an anthropologist who studied human body motion, which he called "kinesics." Birdwhistle was able to demonstrate that no facial expression, stance or body position conveys an identical meaning in all societies. Consider the gestures which mean "There goes a pretty girl." An Arab strokes his beard, a Southern Italian pulls the lobe of his right ear with his right forefinger and thumb. An American man may make a circle with his right thumb and forefinger and blow a kiss through it (pp. 78–81). This gesture could get you into trouble in Brazil.

Erickson's work with the pantomime technique in hypnosis with Spanish-speaking subjects in Mexico and Venezuela and his experimental work with deaf and dumb subjects (1980, pp. 331–339) showed the importance of body movements in hypnotherapy. He was able to induce trance without verbalization. From this he inferred that "similar suggestions can also be unintentionally given" (p. 339). Thus, it would be extremely important for therapists to understand cultural variations in paralinguistic cues to avoid patient misinterpretations.

Another transcultural interest of Erickson's was his consideration of hypnosis in other countries. When he was editor of the *American Journal of Clinical Hypnosis*, he made a plea to therapists to know the formulations from other parts of the world (Erickson, 1965). For example, he published articles dealing with a reflexological explanation of hypnosis (Akstein, 1965) although he did not share this viewpoint. If you examine the journal since his editorship, which ended in 1968, there have only been two articles published in the transcultural area.

Hypnosis is part of culture as is any other area of modern medicine and reflects different world views. Cultural variations are reflected by the names given to hypnosis, choices of techniques, kinds of trance states elicited, and how we explain them. For example, in many countries in South America and in Spain, the name "hypnosis" has been changed to "sophrology," which is defined as "a state of consciousness characterized by a retreat of oneself (ego), which involves simultaneously a neurovegetative participation in which biologically predominates a partial blocking of the function of the ascending reticular activating system" (Gubel, 1967, p. 250). The favored explanation is reflexological rather than interactive. In countries with a highly mystical world view, professionals would more likely embrace a theory based in neurophysiology which would more easily differentiate "scientific" from "mystical" states. In addition, hypnotic techniques are more authoritarian than permissive to avoid any possible confusion with mystical phenomena.

In Asian, South American, Mexican and Italian cultures, valued authority figures are accorded an extremely high degree of prestige. Erickson (1966) commented that his colleagues from these cultures explained "that only occasionally do they encounter patients who do not accept hypnosis but that these seem to be fairly infrequent. Neither do they understand the emphasis placed upon elaborate techniques for the induction of hypnosis. With this in mind, the straightforward uncomplicated reports of our foreign contributors from various countries can be better appreciated" (p. 173). One example was Chong Tong Mun's (1966) work using hypnosis with Asiatic patients as an adjunct in surgery. Of 48 patients offered hypnosis, 46 entered trance. In those cases, a minimum dosage or no medication was used.

Many hypnotherapists have learned a great deal from the naturally occurring trance manifestations in their countries, most often in the context of shamanism. Kim (1967) compared Korean shamanism and hypnosis. Akstein studied ritual trance in Brazilian Umbanda cults for more than twenty-five years. Impressed by their therapeutic nature, Akstein (1973) developed a nonverbal group trance dancing therapy. Erickson also valued studies of trance behavior in other cultures. His knowledge was incorporated into the work of anthropologists like Margaret Mead, Gregory Bateson, Jane Belo, Maya Deren, and the author. "In 1939 Margaret Mead wrote a two-page letter to Erickson inquiring about hypnosis in relation to trance in primitive cultures. He replied with letters of fourteen pages and seventeen pages... The next year Mead traveled to Michigan to meet Erickson, initiating a friendship that lasted until she died" (Zeig, 1985, p. 19). He helped her review and analyze her films of the spontaneous trances of Balinese dancers. Erickson also incorporated his knowledge of these trances in his therapy. For example, in one demonstration with a subject confined to a wheelchair, Erickson (1979) talked about trance recovery as follows: "You are behaving the way they do in Bali. You're showing a partial awakening, a bit at a time. Sometimes your fingers awaken, your toes, your knees and your fingers, then your hands, your arms, your feet. It's a slow process of body orientation."

A trance therapy which provides many insights to the hypnotherapist is performed in Spiritist psychiatric hospitals in Brazil. My anthropological research in such settings focused on Spiritist trance techniques being used by trained physicians with hospitalized patients and outpatients.*

Spiritist Hospitals in Brazil

Spiritism is a religious philosophical system based on communication with the dead and the belief in reincarnation. The form practiced in Latin America and the Caribbean still uses the codification of a nineteenth century French school teacher, alias Allan Kardec, whose *Book of the Spirits* is still a best seller in Brazil today. Kardec rejected Mesmer's notion of animal magnetism, which held that sickness and health were controlled by the balance of a universal invisible fluid in the human body and that the magnetic power of healing comes through the hands. Kardec believed that this power was due to the action of spirits entering human consciousness during seances. Spiritists still stress the action of "fluids" which they believe are spiritual emanations that surround one's body and affect well-being. They are derived from three sources: the innate spirit, spirits of the dead, and incarnate spirits close to the living. These fluids may be good or bad. An individual surrounded by bad fluids may be sick or troubled. Magnetic passes manipulate bad fluids and replace them with good ones. According to Spiritists, illness may also be caused by (a) *karma*, which

---

*From 1976 to 1982, the author conducted anthropological field work in Brazil in both formal and informal mental health systems throughout the country.

refers to situations incurred in former lifetimes for which we take no responsibility but which cause us problems in this existence; (b) undeveloped mediumship, which includes uncontrolled mental phenomena such as possession, seizures, hallucinations, precognitions, and others; (c) *religious negligence* or the failure to perform rituals dictated by spirit guides or adept mediums; (d) *witchcraft*, or the deliberate intent by one individual to harm another; and (e) *obsession*. While distinguishing obsession from insanity because the latter has an organic cause, the more serious forms of mental illness, according to Kardec, are caused by obsession. He divided obsession into three types: moral, corporal, and physical. Another generally accepted cause of illness is the "evil eye," a folk illness caused by intent glances. Sensitive individuals like mediums or children are particularly vulnerable to these "looks."

Spiritists accept the widely held belief that mental illness may be caused by spiritual factors, and as part of their charity ethic, Spiritist societies have founded Spiritist hospitals which are primarily psychiatric. In many cases the government donated the land and partly finances them under the social security system. These hospitals illustrate the professionalization of Brazilian Spiritists, also visible in the numerous professional Spiritist medical societies, conventions, and courses which they organize.

The hospitals vary in size and medical reputation. Three of the sixteen visited by the author were considered to have the highest psychiatric rating, with a staff of more than 100 workers, personnel in many professions, and resident programs in psychiatry. One was a popular retreat for wealthy patients with luxurious accommodations in a country club atmosphere. In addition to medical facilities, they offer "psychodrama" and Spiritist consultations. Because the larger hospitals are partly government financed, they are subject to inspections which more recently have required them to separate medical from Spiritist treatments. The smaller hospitals, which are not receiving government support, are not scrutinized and can therefore promote more Spiritist activities with inpatients. Physicians who work in these hospitals are not necessarily Spiritists. Even those who are not recognize the warmth and humanitarian treatment given to the mentally ill. Spiritist hospitals compare favorably to the large state institutions often called "factories for the insane." In going through medical records, spiritual diagnoses are often combined with psychiatric ones—depression and spiritual obsession, alcoholism in family; extreme exhaustion, incorporation (by spirits); separation from spouse, witchcraft.

According to most Spiritist psychiatrists with whom I spoke, upwards of 70% of all mental illnesses are caused by spirits. They believe the mentally ill are mediums or "sensitives" and thus redefine psychosis or neurosis into paranormal behavior. They perform a culture-specific therapy taken from Kardecian Spiritism called *de-obsession* in which they claim to transform pathological phenomena into paranormal phenomena. Spiritist psychiatrist Eliezer Mendes (1980), trained in medicine in Bahia, works with recuperated patients or mediums whom he trains to "capture" the symptom of the patient and then expell it. For example, he treats epileptic patients without medication by placing the epileptic together with the medium and allowing the mediums to "capture" the patient's convulsions, which supposedly leaves the patient feeling well.

One case example observed by the author in August 1983 was Luis, a twenty-five-year-old schizophrenic drug addict who spent the last ten years of his life in and out of mental hospitals. According to his mother, he was often found naked on the streets, and he went through periodic rages during which he broke objects in the house. She finally took him to Dr. Mendes. Mendes placed Luis on the floor with mediums on all sides of him—holding each hand, touching his head and feet. One medium received the spirit causing the boy's aggression. She writhed on the floor, crying out in vile language as Luis looked on. Luis' mother and the other patients tried to quiet her. Other mediums received spirits which were said to represent different negative forces in Luis' personality, including the self-destructive and hurtful. Luis spoke with these mediums in an interaction directed by Dr. Mendes. These spirits were then educated and told to progress and to attain light. Like an ethnodrama, the mediums act out other selves before the client and are then banished symbolically (Richeport, 1985b).

Playing alternate selves in trance, an indirect form of expression, adapts well to Latin American culture. Generally we think of Latin Americans as explosive and emotionally expressive. However, for many people, hostility is expressed directly only as a last resort. Negative emotions and direct confrontations are avoided because they defy the important cultural values of dignity, honor, and shame. One explanation for the popularity of mediumship trance behavior in informal and formal healing systems may be that it banishes shame and guilt by placing the blame on external or supernatural forces.

Although Spiritist psychiatry provides an excellent opportunity for anthropological research, particularly for its professionalization of an informal healing system, I want to clarify Erickson's views on professionals such as Mendes, as expressed by his wife Elizabeth:

> I know Milton felt VERY EMPHATICALLY that whereas scientists and therapists should study, and when appropriate, *utilize* altered states of consciousness, control of autonomic functions, ways of looking at reality as developed in different cultures—that the bottom line

should be to do it as a scientist—not to join the religion as a true believer, or to buy the whole package of fringe groups. Milton respected David Akstein, M.D., highly for keeping the interpretation and control strictly scientific, while utilizing but not joining the belief system. Milton worked VERY hard all his life to keep hypnosis on a strict scientific level. He had NO respect for people calling themselves scientists and falling for past life regressions, out of body experiences, auras, energy flow from laying on of hands, thought projection, intra-uterine recollections and all of the rest of the "paranormal" range accepted as such without attempting naturalistic explanation, which are adequate, ranging from subconscious interpretation of minimal cues through inadequate controls, misinterpretation, self-deception, faulty reporting, to outright deliberate deception and charlatanism. (E. Erickson, personal communication, August 19, 1986).

Culturally Appropriate Hypnotherapy

What happens when a patient meets a therapist from a different culture? Without knowing the culture, therapists may misinterpret symptoms, incorrectly reading linguistic and kinesic cues. Garrison (1982, p. 82) asked: What might happen when Spiritist patients enter the mental health system? If the doctor is Anglo, the patients would not express Spiritist beliefs and would be judged as "lacking insight," "somatizing," or "denying" because they do not communicate "spiritual" concerns. If they do talk about spiritual causes would they be considered "delusions of persecution" or would "spirit guides" be judged as "delusions of grandeur"?

Therapists may give advice counter to cultural mores or values. It is important to understand the patient's perceptions of causation and preferred treatments. For example, weight loss and fever most worry Hispanics and "hot and cold" categories of foods and medicines should be considered in remediation. Chinese and Haitian patients expect dietary changes as part of medical treatments. Alternative healers are consulted by many ethnic groups in the United States from the less formally organized "therapeutic women" among Italian Americans and root workers by some blacks, to the more formally organized Haitian Voodoo priests, Mexican *curanderos* and Puerto Rican *espiritistas* (Harwood, 1981, p. 494). Knowing their styles of practice provides important clues to cultural expectations.

Therapists might consider the following issues in performing culturally appropriate hypnotherapy:

Authoritarian vs. Indirect Approach

Are patients more comfortable with an authoritarian or permissive approach? Latin American and Oriental patients expect authoritarian, paternal, experts, who use all of the social cues of their profession. These patients expect a vertical, unequal relationship and expect to be told what is wrong and what to do about it. Kim (1983, p. 238), citing Nguyen, tells the story of a Vietnamese patient who went to a psychiatrist who said to him, "I would like you to cooperate with me." The patient never again returned. The statement was a shock since cooperation assumed equal status. Because these groups have a range of shamanistic healers who specialize in giving advice, when advice is not given by the professional, this may be interpreted as indifference or not caring.

An Ericksonian directive approach would be compatible with these cultural expectations. This is illustrated in the case of a Lebanese stutterer (Richeport, 1985a, pp. 541–546) in which Erickson capitalized on the expectation of an authoritarian figure to assure patient and family compliance with his therapeutic prescriptions, which were, incidentally, contrary to the cultural ideals of paternal authority, dependence on family, and inequality among the sexes. Erickson regarded this patient's cultural patterns as maladaptive in urban American society and as adding to the patient's problems, yet he utilized the authoritarian cultural pattern to his advantage.

Another example of an Ericksonian approach which turns a cultural premise into a strength is described by Kim (1983, p. 238) for Asian Americans. Giving initial intimacy to a stranger (therapist) is a sign of lack of self-control and a cause for shame, not only to oneself but to one's family. In accord with an Ericksonian directive approach and cultural expectations, the therapist might direct the patient to withhold information and not to trust the therapist-stranger until such time as he or she is ready to do so. After all, this is only the first interview. Here we have an example of a paradoxical directive which is culturally syntonic. Ignorance of this cultural premise might lead the therapist to regard the patient as resistant.

Direct or Indirect Communication Styles

In examining other cultural traditions, we find that indirect communication is often more acceptable than direct communication. The ethnodramas in Spiritist psychiatry and parables, storytelling, and metaphors in Oriental traditions are two examples. In this way, direct self-exploration is avoided at the verbal conscious level, and cultural patterns of deflection and avoidance of confrontation to save face can be maintained. Kim (1983, p. 241) gives the example of two taboo areas in Chinese American culture — suicide and sex. Therapists can talk about eating instead of sex, for example, which is more compatible with cultural learning through metaphor, as in the Confucian sayings. Using the familiar style also helps to bypass conscious resistance. Kim has also found it useful to use "reframing" with patients. Relabeling what patients do in a positive way allows them to "save face." If the patient is self-conscious, the therapist might say, "You don't have to talk...perhaps you can learn more by listening and reflecting."

In many instances a direct communication style is warranted. In Latin America and the Caribbean, as mentioned earlier, it has been difficult to differentiate hypnosis from mediumship phenomena within a mystical world view. My observations of hypnotic techniques in Brazil showed that they are directed so as to leave no room for ambiguities to arise which may then be interpreted mystically. For example, when relaxation techniques are used, the hypnotist suggests that each part of the body relax and then gives suggestions for well-being but does not leave time for open-ended suggestions. Ideomotor techniques such as automatic writing or hand levitation are not used as they could easily be interpreted as spirit writing or possession by an external force responsible for the movements. Only in cases where the patient is a medium or a Spiritist believer, and where the doctor felt it appropriate to utilize this system in the therapy for the benefit of the patient, would the trance be permissive enough to allow these expressions (Richeport, 1982, 1985a).

Other guidelines for culturally appropriate hypnotherapy include the degree of personalism or impersonality used, direct or indirect eye contact, and the use of touch, so as not to violate cultural proprieties. The patient should be asked if touch is acceptable. One study in a natural setting showed a great difference in the number of times people touch one another. Forsdale (1974, p. 14) counted the number of times people touched each other in public places in a period of an hour in four different cities and got the following tally: San Juan, Puerto Rico, 180; Paris, France, 110; Gainesville, Florida, 2; and London, England, 0.

If we examine eye contact as it occurs naturally in everyday life we also find cultural differences. Looking directly in Anglo culture means trust, attentiveness, and courtesy. In the Hispanic Caribbean, on the other hand, among members of the same sex, looking directly while speaking means challenge or suspicion, while looking directly at a member of the opposite sex while speaking is part of the seduction and courting ritual. The Anglo who listens to an eye-shifting Hispanic gets the impression that he or she is not paying attention or showing interest. These cultural nonverbal patterns are brought to therapy. A female Hispanic patient may be afraid to send provocative messages to a male therapist, for example, and may not look at him. This, in turn, may be interpreted by the therapist as resistance or lack of cooperation (Nine-Curt, 1983).

Observation of the ordinary cultural context was very important to Erickson's understanding of the ethnic background of patients. However, he always considered intra-ethnic differences and treated each patient as a unique individual.

Erickson as a Shaman

Years ago I gave Erickson a witchdoctor's mask because I knew that he appreciated anthropology and primitive art. At that time, at least consciously, I did not think of him as a witchdoctor or shaman. Margaret Mead once said to me, "There are very few healers in this world, and Milton is one of them. That is why he can't teach anyone what he does." From cross-cultural observation, it appears that shamans around the world share many commonalities. Utilizing Rossi's (1983) biography, it is possible to describe Erickson as a shaman. Shamans are those people who possess remarkable knowledge and techniques known to restore health and well-being in their communities, where they achieve considerable prestige. Shamans operate in states of nonordinary reality and help others to use other levels of consciousness and the sacred powers within each self (Harner, 1980, p. xi).

Initiation into the Shaman's Calling

Studies of cultures around the world reveal that there are certain factors that lead individuals to become shamans. In some societies, the powers to heal are handed down from one generation to the next. In others, individuals who are physically or emotionally handicapped experience a self-cure through great personal suffering. Society then provides a prestigious role for these nonordinary individuals, to direct their strength and experiential knowledge into helping others. Erickson was struck by polio at seventeen and left totally paralyzed during a time when there were no rehabilitation facilities available for a farm boy. Instead of succumbing, he turned all his handicaps into assets and became a shaman.

Erickson's technique came from his own blood and suffering; his therapeutic originality evolved out of life and death efforts to cope with his own congenital deficiencies and crippling physical illnesses... Patients could sense on many levels that Erickson's therapeutic skill came from genuine personal experience and knowledge. He truly was the wounded physician who through healing himself had learned how to heal others. (Rossi, 1983, p. 58)

Transition and Transformation

In anthropology, Van Gennep (1960) described the ceremonies that accompany life's crises as "rites of passage" in which individuals pass through three major stages: separation, transition, and incorporation. "For groups as well as individuals, life itself means to separate and to be reunited, to change form and condition, to die and to be reborn. It is to act and to cease, to wait and rest, and then to begin acting again, but in a different way. And there are always new thresholds to cross: the thresholds of summer and winter, of a season or a year, of a month or a night; thresholds of birth, adolescence, maturity, and old age" (pp. 189–190). In the first stage the individual is detached or separated by his or her condition. During the transitional or "liminal" period the individual's status is ambiguous with few attributes of either past or future. In the third phase, the passage is consumated; his or her status is clearly defined. The individual is reaggregated into the group as a different person. These stages are similar to Wallace's (1969) concept of "mazeway resynthesis" which he originally applied to the Seneca Indian prophet Handsome Lake. The "resynthesis" is the restructuring of learned cognitions during periods of stress and intense emotional conflict, often occurring via hallucinatory trance experiences as therapeutic responses.*

Erickson's transition of self-discovery and self-help is an inspiring tale of recovery, of personal and social transformation. Much of his knowledge came through hallucinatory trance experiences. For example, Erickson learned that by exercising the idea of a movement, by activating real sense memories, he was able to restimulate his sensory-motor coordination to recovery. This experience provided the basis of his understanding of ideomotor and ideosensor responses in hypnosis.

> One day his family left him alone tied to a rocking chair. The chair was somewhere in the middle of the room with Milton in it, looking longingly at the window, wishing he were closer to it so that he could at least have the pleasure of gazing out at the farm. As he sat there, apparently immobile, wishing and wondering, *he suddenly became*

---

*Richeport (1975, 1985c) applied this model together with Rossi's (1973) model of "psychological shocks and creative moments in psychotherapy" to analyze the life histories of Puerto Rican and Brazilian Spiritists as they learn to become mediums.

aware that his chair began to rock slightly... In the weeks and months that followed, Milton foraged through his sense memories to try to relearn how to move. He would stare for hours at his hand, for example, and try to recall how his fingers had felt when grasping a pitchfork. Bit by bit he found his fingers beginning to twitch and move in tiny, uncoordinated ways. He persisted until the movements became larger and until he could consciously control them. (Rossi, 1983, p. 12)

When Erickson was a young college student and dependent on crutches, he decided to make a ten-week canoe trip alone. The story of this heroic journey is like an initiation rite into pain and hardship that few primitive tribesmen would brave. It turned a frail crippled boy into a robust man with a limp (Rossi, 1983, pp. 14–15).

The stories of Erickson's constant testing and experimentation with his own unconscious led him to the challenge of writing editorials for a local Wisconsin newspaper while still in college. He would go to sleep at 10:30 p.m. and set his alarm for 1:00 a.m. planning to type out the editorials. When he awoke in the morning, he found the typewritten material but had no memory of getting up and writing. He placed the material in the editor's box without reading it, and kept a carbon copy. When the editorials were published, he did not recognize the writing as his own, and only knew so by consulting the copies. These experiments led to Erickson's knowledge of somnambulistic activity and hypnotic amnesia and to the realization that "there was a lot more in my head than I realized" (Rossi, 1983, p. 17). These kinds of naturalistic experiments, although they might seem supernatural to many, finally led to Erickson's "incorporation" into the role of physician or shaman. This resynthesis or cognitive transformation occurred after numerous altered states experiments where meaning complexes were free to rearrange themselves as he learned to trust his unconscious.

Styles of Practice

Shamans' reputations are built up from their training, experience, and reported successes which enable them to build clients' expectations or faith in the healer. While this may seem an insignificant point, anthropologists have documented the power of expectation on the negative side to produce the classical "voodoo death" syndrome (Cannon, 1942; Lex, 1974). In societies where beliefs in witchcraft are prevalent, when people believe that they have been hexed, they may be regarded as dead by the community and thus isolated from social life. They become so convinced of the impending doom that they stop drinking and eating, acting as though they were already dead. The sympathetic nervous system becomes so disorganized that within a few hours it leads to a drop in blood volume and blood pressure with irreparable damage to circulatory organs. Resulting deaths reveal no apparent lesions. On the positive side, faith, hope, and expectancy can bring about profound changes leading to healing, creativity, and personal growth.

Erickson, like other shamans, noted his former successes in many seemingly impossible situations, such as in the case of the cancer patient who lived long enough to see her son graduate (Erickson, 1979) or the ugly fat girl who finds her prince charming (Erickson, 1979).

Shamans are members of a community. People know where they live, know their families, and know where to find them in times of need. This is in contrast to most therapists, who hide behind the veil of the fifty-minute session and are never seen before or after. They seem to be answering machines without spouses or children. Erickson saw patients in his home where they watched the family in their daily routines and development.

> That humble home office on Cypress Street was a humanizing experience for all who crossed its threshold. Patients constantly tripped over agreeable dogs and children in the family living room which also doubled as a waiting room. A basset hound named "Roger" was so relaxed lying in the middle of the floor that patients often fell into reverie and trance just by watching him. Thus Erickson felt this work was made easier. Indeed, it wasn't so much a matter of doctor-patient relationship as of family-patient relationships. Children would draw pictures for patients and little sweet-nothing gifts of sentiment would be exchanged (Rossi, 1983, pp. 42–43).
>
> Although personal characteristics of shamans vary from culture to culture, characteristics of absolute self confidence, charisma, and mystery seem to be a shaman's requisites. The mystery derives from the secrets they gain privy to in altered states of consciousness. Erickson said that he usually went into trance with a difficult case (Rossi, 1983, p. 25).

Myths and Rituals

Erickson's stories about his family are the shamanic myths which permit visualization and teach about healthy development. Zeig (1980, pp. 25–26) has described some of the functions of these stories as follows: They are nonthreatening, engaging, and foster independence. They can be used to bypass natural resistance to change, control the relationship by throwing the individuals off balance while they try to make sense out of it, and create confusion and promote hypnotic responsiveness. They make the presented idea more memorable.

Closely tied to myths, anecdotes, teaching tales, as they have been called, are shamanic rituals. The first ritual is for a patient to get to the shaman—the pilgrimage to Mecca, Lourdes, the Spiritist center, or Phoenix, Arizona. The expense and travel itself may be a sacrifice and hardship. Shamans then prescribe rituals in a direct and forceful manner, impressing upon the patient that executing the ritual will improve their condition. Erickson made patients promise that they would carry out his rituals, which were usually less formidable than keeping the problem. He taught his students, "You should involve your patient in your form of therapy. Get the patient to do something, You don't just explain" (Erickson, 1979). "The ideology and ritual supply the patient with a conceptual framework for organizing his chaotic, mysterious, and vague distress and give him a plan of action, helping him to regain a sense of direction and mastery and to resolve his inner conflicts" (Frank, cited in Kiev, 1964, p. 8).

Rituals also serve to put behavior under control by limiting undesirable behaviors in time and space. Unwanted spirit possessions are, for example, encouraged, but only in front of an altar or in a center, and discouraged in ordinary settings. Shamans' rituals may be considered under the "displacement of cathexis" (Beahrs, 1971, p. 239). Patients are given something new to displace psychic energy from the original problems. It may be the ritual of learning a new hobby or skill or performing a particular task. It appears almost magical because there is no attempt to uncover underlying interpretations but rather a redirection of psychic energy into more constructive outlets.

Research Possibilities in Hypnosis from the Transcultural Perspective

Most phenomena of hypnosis can be studied from the transcultural perspective. This provides the opportunity to see the phenomena occurring naturalistically in two or more settings simultaneously. A few clinicians have already expressed an interest in cross-cultural data. Rossi (1986) has questioned whether healers capitalize on ultradian cycles in their work. Gindhart (1982) found it useful to study hand postures in my Afro-Spiritist films to see how they facilitate trance induction.

The Brazilian Spiritist movement suggests research opportunities to study hypnosis with psychotic and epileptic patients. Since many of the mediumship trance techniques are reproducible in hypnosis, we are looking at analogous states. Erickson described them as "the same psychophysiological states with different understandings" (Personal communication, n.d.). In the practices I have discussed, trance techniques were used without medication. Does the de-obsession technique function with patients in crisis? Can hypnosis treat grand mal epilepsy without medication? Gravitz (1979) reported the successful use of hypnosis with one case of grand mal seizures. Because automatic writing is used in Spiritism, researchers might be interested in these expressions in and out of trance and as a diagnostic tool.

Considering the fact that so many ethnic populations consult alternate healing systems which employ trance techniques, studying their styles of practice would contribute to understanding the ways rapport is established in the therapeutic process and therapeutic efficacy is achieved in healing.

References

Akstein, D. (1965). The induction of hypnosis in the light of reflexology. *American Journal of Clinical Hypnosis, 2*, 281–300.

Akstein, D. (1973). *Hipnologia* (Vol. 1). Rio de Janeiro: Hypnos.

Beahrs, J. O. (1971). The hypnotic psychotherapy of Milton H. Erickson. *American Journal of Clinical Hypnosis, 14*, 73–90.

Birdwhistle, R. L. (1970). *Kinesics and context: Essays on body motion communication.* Philadelphia: University of Pennsylvania.

Cannon, W. B. (1942). "Voodoo" death. *American Anthropologist, 44*, 169–181.

Chong, T. M. (1966). The use of hypnosis as an adjunct in surgery. *American Journal of Clinical Hypnosis, 8*(3), 178–180.

Erickson, M. H. (1965). Editor's comment. *American Journal of Clinical Hypnosis, 2*, 281.

Erickson, M. H. (1966). Editor's comment. *American Journal of Clinical Hypnosis, 3*, 173.

Erickson, M. H. (1979). Teaching seminar, December 11–23, 1979, at 1201 West Hayward, Phoenix, Arizona.

Erickson, M. H. (1980). *The collected papers of Milton H. Erickson: Vol. 1. The nature of hypnosis and suggestion* (E. L. Rossi, Ed.). New York: Irvington.

Forsdale, L. (1974). *Non-verbal communication.* New York: Harcourt-Brace Jovanovich.

Garrison, V. (1982). *Folk healing systems as elements in the community support system of psychiatric patients.* In U. Rueveni, R. V. Speck, & J. L. Speck (Eds.), *Therapeutic interventions: Healing strategies for human systems* (pp. 58–95). New York: Human Sciences Press.

Gindhart, L. R. (1982). *A clinical note on the use of hand posture in trance induction and implications for non-verbal communication.* Unpublished manuscript, Indianapolis, Indiana.

Gravitz, M. (1979). Hypnotherapeutic management of epileptic behavior. *American Journal of Clinical Hypnosis, 21*, 282–284.

Gubel, I. (1967). Sophrology. *American Journal of Clinical Hypnosis, 9*, 247–251.

Harner, M. (1980). *The way of the shaman. A guide to power and healing.* San Francisco: Harper & Row.

Harwood, A. (Ed.). (1981). *Ethnicity and medical care.* Cambridge, MA: Harvard University Press.

Kiev, A. (Ed.). (1964). *Magic, faith, and healing.* New York: Free Press.

Kim, S. C. (1983). Ericksonian hypnotic framework for Asian-Americans. *American Journal of Clinical Hypnosis, 25,* 235–241.

Kim, W. (1967). Shamanism and hypnosis. *American Journal of Clinical Hypnosis, 9,* 193–197.

Lefley, H. P. (1984). Cross-cultural training for mental health professionals: Effects on the delivery of services. *Hospital & Community Psychiatry, 35,* 1227–1229.

Lefley, H. P., & Bestman, E. W. (1984). Community mental health and minorities: A multi-ethnic approach. In S. Sue & T. Moore (Eds.), *The pluralistic society: A community mental health perspective* (pp. 116–148). New York: Human Sciences Press.

Lefley, H. P., & Pedersen, P. B. (Eds.). (1986). *Cross-cultural training for mental health professionals.* Springfield, IL: Charles C Thomas.

Lex, B. W. (1974). Voodoo death: New thoughts on an old explanation. *American Anthropologist, 76,* 818–823.

Mendes, E. (1980). *Psicotranse.* Sao Paulo: Editora Pensamento.

Nine-Curt, C. J. (1983). *Intercultural interaction in the Hispanic-Anglo ESL classroom from a non-verbal perspective.* Unpublished manuscript, University of Puerto Rico, Rio Piedras.

Richeport (Michtom), M. (1975). *Becoming a medium: The role of trance in Puerto Rican Spiritism as an avenue to mazeway resynthesis.* Ann Arbor: University of Michigan Press.

Richeport, M. (1982). Erickson's contribution to anthropology. In J. Zeig (Ed.), *Ericksonian approaches to hypnosis and psychotherapy* (pp. 371–390). New York: Brunner/Mazel.

Richeport, M. (1985a). The importance of anthropology in psychotherapy. In J. Zeig (Ed.), *Ericksonian psychotherapy: Vol. 1. Structures* (pp. 537–552). New York: Brunner/Mazel.

Richeport, M. (1985b). *Macumba, trance and spirit healing* [16 mm Film, 45 min.]. New York: Filmmakers Library.

Richeport, M. (1985c). *Terapias alternativas num bairro de Natal: Estudo na antropologia medica.* Natal, Brazil: Editora Universitaria.

Rossi, E. L. (1973). Psychological shocks and creative moments in psychotherapy. *American Journal of Clinical Hypnosis, 16,* 9–22.

Rossi, E. L. (1983). Milton H. Erickson: A biographical sketch. In E. L. Rossi, M. O. Ryan, & F. Sharp (Eds.), *Healing in hypnosis: The seminars, workshops, and lectures of Milton H. Erickson* (Vol. 1, pp. 1–59). New York: Irvington.

Rossi, E. L. (1986). Hypnosis and ultradian rhythms. In B. Zilbergeld et al. (Eds.), *Hypnosis questions and answers* (pp. 17–21). New York: Norton.

Van Gennep, A. (1960). *The rites of passage.* Chicago: University of Chicago Press.

Wallace, A. (1969). *Culture and personality.* New York: Random House.

Weidman, H. H. (1978). *The Miami health ecology project report: A statement on ethnicity and health* (Vol. 1). Miami: University of Miami.

Weidman, H. H. (Ed.). (1979). The transcultural perspective in health and illness. *Social Science & Medicine, 13B*(2), 85–167.

Weidman, H. H. (1983). Research, service, and training aspects of clinical anthropology: An institutional overview. In D. B. Shimkin & P. Golde (Eds.), *Clinical anthropology: A new approach to American health problems?* (pp. 119–153). Lanham, MD: University Press of America.

Weidman, H. H. (1985). *The transcultural view.* Talk presented at the Workshop on Afro-Spiritist Trance Healing, University of Miami School of Medicine, Miami, Florida, June 22.

Zeig, J. K. (Ed.). (1980). *A teaching seminar with Milton H. Erickson.* New York: Brunner/Mazel.

Zeig, J. K. (1985). *Experiencing Erickson: An introduction to the man and his work.* New York: Brunner/Mazel.